GCSE Mathematics Numerical Crosswords

Higher Tier

Written for the GCSE 9-1 Course

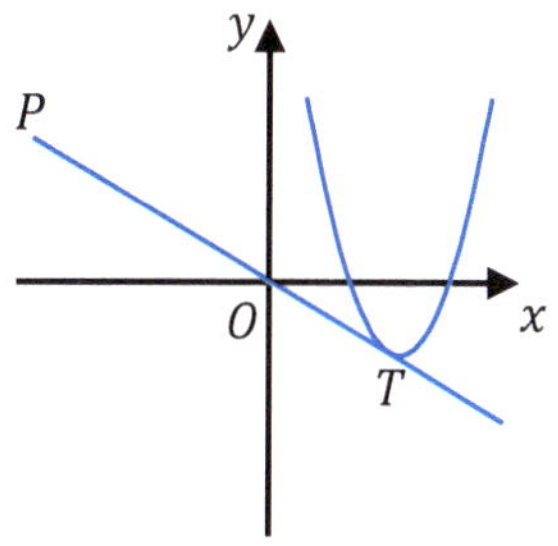

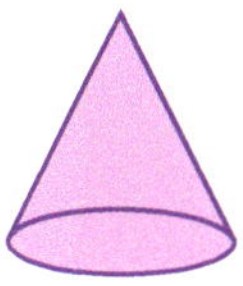

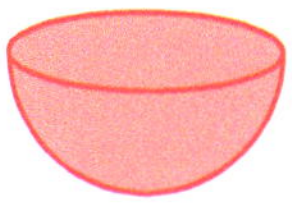

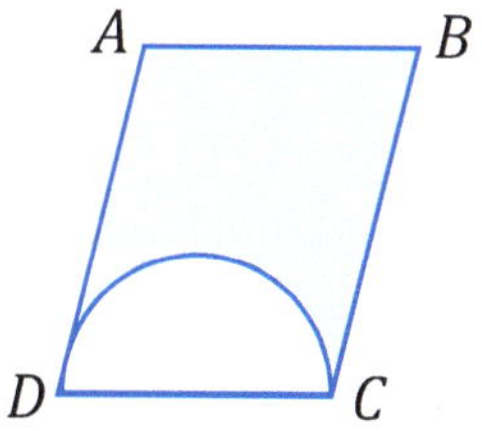

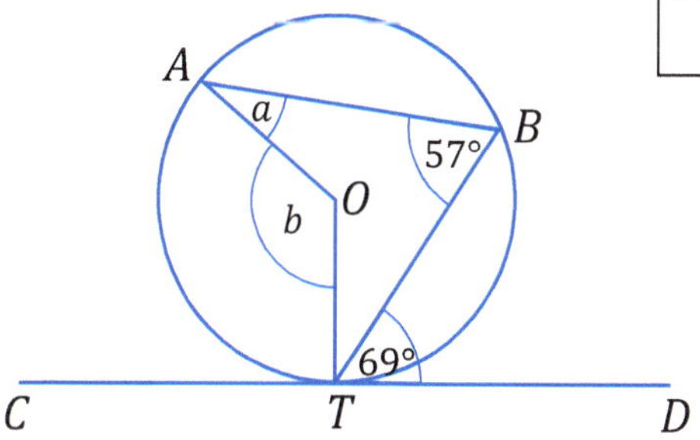

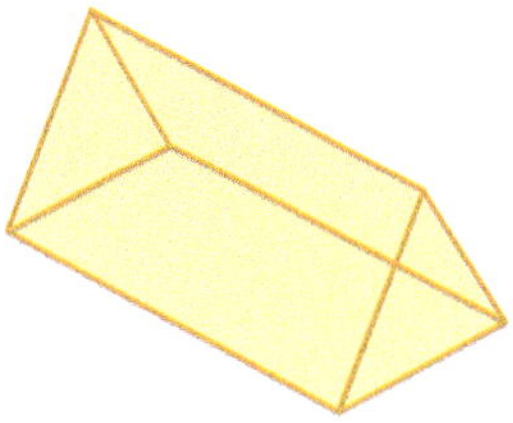

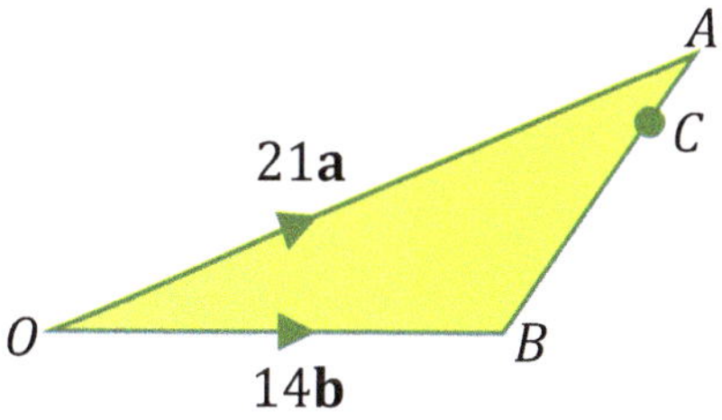

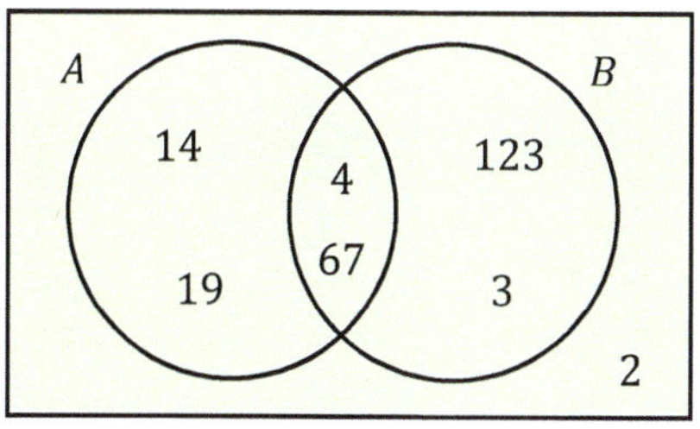

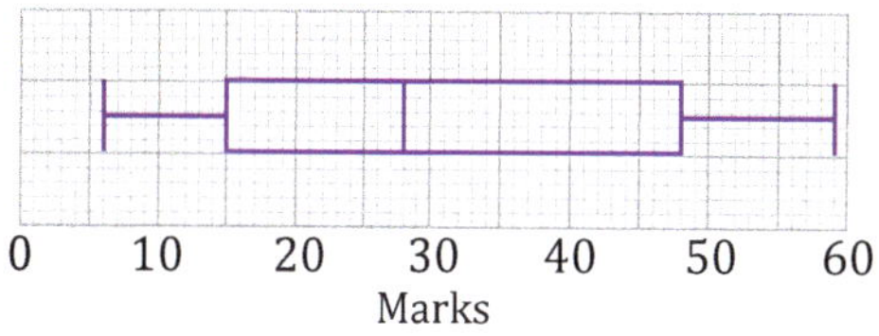

BY IAN WINKWORTH

Copyright ©Ian Winkworth, 2018

Published by The University of Buckingham Press
Yeomanry House
Hunter Street
Buckingham MK18 1EG
www.ubpl.co.uk

All rights reserved. No reproduction, copy or transmission of this publication may be made without written permission.

Except for the quotation of short passages for the purposes of research or private study, or criticism and review, no part of this publication may be reproduced, stored in a retrieval system, copied or transmitted, in any form or by any means, electronic, mechanical, photocopying, recording or otherwise, now known or hereafter invented, save with written permission or in accordance with the provisions of the Copyright, Design and Patents Act 1988, or under terms of any licence permitting limited copying issued by the publisher.

This book is sold subject to the condition that it shall not, by way of trade or otherwise, be lent, resold, hired out, or otherwise circulated without the publisher's prior consent in any form of binding or cover other than that in which it is published and without a similar condition including this condition being imposed on the subsequent purchaser.

Any person who does any unauthorised act in relation to this publication may be liable to criminal prosecution and civil claims for damages.

ISBN 978-1-912500-06-2

Introduction

GCSE Mathematics Numerical Crosswords bring fun into learning and revising Mathematics in a focused, enjoyable and succinct format. The content of this book is based on the GCSE Mathematics grade 9-1 higher tier course with fully worked examination standard examples and complete explanations for all questions. The structure of the book means that readers will cover each of the five key GCSE Mathematics areas quickly, with chapters on:

1. Number
2. Algebra
3. Ratio, Proportion and Rates of Change
4. Geometry and Measures
5. Probability and Statistics

At the end of each chapter is a consolidation crossword which revisits the key themes of the section.

Guidance on how to use this book

Read each crossword clue carefully and have a pen, paper and calculator ready to work through each problem. Once you have the answer to the clue write it in the crossword grid. Do not include any units (e.g. centimetres, kilograms, degrees etc.) when writing answers in the crossword grid, just write in the numerical solution. Unless stated, always write the answer to the last calculation for each clue in the grid. If you are unsure on how to answer a question use the examples on the right page of each crossword to help you. In the back of the book are full solutions, including explanations to every clue.

Contents

Chapter 1: Number

Crossword 1 - Operations and Standard Form 8

Crossword 2 - Factors, Multiples and Listing Strategies 10

Crossword 3 - Indices and Surds 12

Crossword 4 - Fractions, Decimals and Percentages 14

Crossword 5 - Measures, Approximation and Estimation 16

Crossword 6 - Chapter 1 Consolidation Crossword 18

Chapter 2: Algebra

Crossword 7 - Algebraic Methods 22

Crossword 8 - Linear Equations and Inequalities 24

Crossword 9 - Straight Line Graphs 26

Crossword 10 - Quadratic Equations and Inequalities 28

Crossword 11 - Functions and Transformations 30

Crossword 12 - Iterations, Sequences and Real-Life Graphs 32

Crossword 13 - Chapter 2 Consolidation Crossword 34

Chapter 3: Ratio, Proportion and Rates of Change

Crossword 14 - Ratio, Similarity and Proportionality 38

Crossword 15 - Rates of Change and Compound Measures 40

Crossword 16 - Chapter 3 Consolidation Crossword 42

Chapter 4: Geometry and Measures

Crossword 17 - Angles, Congruency, Area and Perimeter 46

Crossword 18 - Vectors and Transformations 48

Crossword 19 - Circles 50

Crossword 20 - Trigonometry 52

Crossword 21 - 3D Shapes, Surface Area and Volume 54

Crossword 22 - Chapter 4 Consolidation Crossword 56

Chapter 5: Probability and Statistics

Crossword 23 - Probability 60

Crossword 24 - Statistics 62

Crossword 25 - Chapter 5 Consolidation Crossword 64

Crossword Solutions 67

Chapter 1
Number

Crossword 1: Operations and Standard Form

Across

1. Calculate $-8 + (-17) - (-52)$
3. Calculate $\dfrac{7^2 \times (3+7)}{8 - (\sqrt{9} \times 2)}$
6. Which one of the three symbols below should be placed in the empty box to make the statement true? Write the number underneath the correct symbol in the grid

   $-5 + 12 \; \square \; 27 \div 3$

=	>	<
61	62	63

7. Which one of the four symbols below should be placed in the empty box to make the statement true? Write the number underneath the correct symbol in the grid

   $-4 - 15 \; \square \; (2 \times -3) + 1$

≥	≠	>	=
125	115	165	145

9. A webpage received 29 views per day for 30 days. How many views did the webpage receive in total during the 30 days?
10. The temperature in City A is $-5°C$ and the temperature in City B is $17°C$. By how many °C is the temperature higher in City B than in City A?

Down

2. Work out $(-5 \times 51) \times (-7 - (-4))$
4. What is the reciprocal of 0.002?
5. Which one of the four symbols below should be placed in the empty box to make the statement true? Write the number underneath the correct symbol in the grid

   $-3 \times -5 \times 2 \; \square \; 14 + 3 - (-13)$

≠	≤	>	<
11	41	31	21

8. A group of twenty thousand people won a lottery jackpot of £2.94 million. The money was split equally between all individuals in the group. How many pounds did each person receive?
9. A football team is awarded 6 points for a win, 2 points for a draw and 0 points for a loss. In a 30-game season the team won 11 games, lost 11 games and drew the rest. How many points in total did the team have at the end of the season?
10. If $0.12 \times 2.25 = 0.27$, what is 1.2×22.5?
11. If $400 \times 249 = 99600$, what is 40×24.9?
12. If $\dfrac{198000}{45} = 4400$, what is 44×4.5?
13. The length of a rectangle is (3.5×10^4) millimetres. Its width is a seventh of its length. What is the area of the rectangle in square metres? Give your answer as an ordinary number

Across continued

11. Write 9.717×10^3 as an ordinary number
14. Calculate $(1.105 \times 10^3) - (9.78 \times 10^2)$, giving your answer as an ordinary number
15. Calculate $(3.04 \times 10^3) \div (5 \times 10^{-2})$, giving your answer as an ordinary number

Down continued

14. Express 81,432,156,302 in standard form (i.e. $a \times 10^n$) and write the value of n in the grid

Operations

Rules

+ and − rules		
+ +	=	+
+ −	=	−
− +	=	−
− −	=	+

× rules		
+ × +	=	+
+ × −	=	−
− × +	=	−
− × −	=	+

÷ rules		
+ ÷ +	=	+
+ ÷ −	=	−
− ÷ +	=	−
− ÷ −	=	+

Order of operations	
1	Brackets
2	Indices
3	Division
4	Multiplication
5	Addition
6	Subtraction

Reciprocal of $n = \frac{1}{n}$

Examples	Solutions
Calculate -3×6	$-3 \times 6 = -18$
Calculate $\frac{10^2 + -1}{-3 \times -11}$	$\frac{10^2 + -1}{33} = \frac{100 - 1}{33} = \frac{99}{33} = 3$
What is the reciprocal of 0.1?	$\frac{1}{0.1} = 10$
Which symbol ($>, <, =, \leq$) should be placed in the empty box to make the following statement true? $19 - (-8) \, \square \, 9 \times 2$	Left-hand side $= 19 - (-8) = 19 + 8 = 27$ which is $>$ the right-hand side $= 9 \times 2 = 18$
If $57 \times 412 = 23484$, what is 5.7×4.12?	As $6 \times 4 = 24$, the answer must be 23.484

Standard Form

Standard form format

$a \times 10^n$ where $1 \leq a < 10$ and n is an integer

Examples	Solutions
Write 4.701×10^4 as an ordinary number	47010
Write 0.0025 in standard form	2.5×10^{-3}
Calculate $(8.7 \times 10^3) + (1.2 \times 10^2)$	$8700 + 120 = 8820$
Calculate $(1.5 \times 10^4) \times (2 \times 10^{-3})$	$15000 \times 0.002 = 30$

Crossword 2: Factors, Multiples and Listing Strategies

Across

1. What is the 7th multiple of 24?
3. Write 80 as the product of its prime factors. Then multiply the largest prime factor of 80 by 25 and write the result in the grid
5. Write 96 as the product of its prime factors in index form $a^n \times b$ where $n > 1$. Then multiply the value of n by 9 and write the result in the grid
7. Add 67 to the highest common factor (HCF) of 42 and 56
9. The prime factors of 18 and 30 are shown in the Venn diagram below. Using this information, multiply the lowest common multiple (LCM) of 18 and 30 by 11

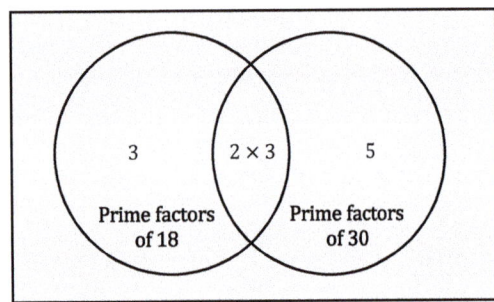

10. Expressed as a product of its prime factors $78 = 2 \times 3 \times 13$. What is the LCM of 78 and 286?
12. If $x = 2^3 \times 3 \times 5^2$, $y = \frac{3}{4}x$ and $z = \frac{x}{10}$, determine the HCF of y and z
13. What whole number between 20 and 95 is a multiple of 16 and 24 and is also a factor of 768?

Down

1. Sum of all factors of 85
2. Sum of all factors of 44
4. Complete the factor tree below to find the value of x

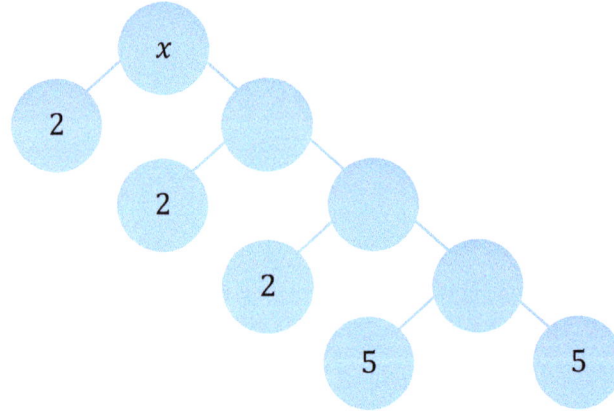

6. Multiply the HCF of 66 and 110 by 272
8. LCM of 20 and 36
11. Jason sips some water every 9 minutes and Anna sips some water every 12 minutes. They both sip some water at exactly 10 am. How many seconds after 10 am will they both next sip some water at the same time?
12. What whole number between 300 and 400 is a multiple of 15 and is exactly divisible by 8?
14. Heng has 2 T-shirts, 5 pairs of trousers and 83 caps. An outfit consists of one of each of the three items of clothing. How many different outfits does Heng have?

Across continued

16. Herbert has 8 different toys. He gives 1 to Marilyn, 1 to Frank and 1 to David. In how many different ways can Herbert do this?
17. Dianne picks a 3-digit integer which is greater than 199. The number is also a multiple of 2. How many different 3-digit numbers can Dianne pick?

Down continued

15. Rachel has 3 different DVDs, 4 different CDs and 6 different books. Her evening consists of either:
    a) watching a DVD and playing a CD, or
    b) watching a DVD, playing a CD and reading a book

    How many different ways can Rachel do this?

Factors and Multiples

Examples	Solutions	
What is the 4th multiple of 6?	$4 \times 6 = 24$	
Find all the factors of 36	Check to see if 1, 2, 3, 4, 5, 6, 7, 8, … are factors of 36. Stop when a factor is repeated. All factors of 36 are shown to the right in pairs. $(1 \times 36), (2 \times 18), (3 \times 12), (4 \times 9)$ and (6×6) are factor pairs. As 6 is repeated we stop looking for pairs at this point. Factors of 36 are 1, 2, 3, 4, 6, 9, 12, 18, 36	1|36 4|9 2|18 5|- 3|12 6|6
Write 20 as the product of its prime factors	$20 = 2 \times 2 \times 5 = 2^2 \times 5$ in index form	
What is the highest common factor (HCF) of 10 and 50?	Product of prime factors of 10 = 2×5. Product of prime factors of 50 = $2 \times 5 \times 5$. HCF = product of shared prime factors (in red) = $2 \times 5 = 10$	
What is the lowest common multiple (LCM) of 40 and 92?	Product of prime factors of 40 = $2 \times 2 \times 2 \times 5$. Product of prime factors of 92 = $2 \times 2 \times 23$. HCF = product of shared prime factors (in red) = $2 \times 2 = 4$. LCM = HCF × remaining prime factors = $4 \times 2 \times 5 \times 23 = 920$	

Listing Strategies

Examples	Solutions
Laura has 9 different scarfs and 6 different pairs of glasses. How many different combinations of the scarfs and glasses can she wear?	$9 \times 6 = 54$
A group of children consists of 5 boys and 7 girls. A team is to be chosen from the group of either: a) 2 boys and 1 girl, or b) 2 girls and 1 boy How many different teams can be formed?	2 boys and 1 girl, $5 \times 4 \times 7 = 140$. 2 girls and 1 boy, $7 \times 6 \times 5 = 210$. Total team options: $140 + 210 = 350$
Graham picks a 4-digit integer which is greater than 5999. The number is also a multiple of 10. How many different 4-digit numbers can Graham pick?	There are 4 options for the 1st digit (6 to 9), 10 options for each of the 2nd and 3rd digits (0 to 9) and 1 option for the 4th digit (0). Therefore, there are $4 \times 10 \times 10 \times 1 = 400$ different numbers

Crossword 3: Indices and Surds

Across

1. Evaluate $\sqrt{8} \times \sqrt{18}$
2. Express $(14 - \sqrt{7})(6 + \sqrt{7})$ in the form $a + b\sqrt{7}$. Then determine the product of values a and b and write the result in the grid
4. Write $\sqrt{128}$ in the form of $a\sqrt{2}$. Then add the value of a to 47 and write the result in the grid
5. Evaluate $\frac{\sqrt{180}}{\sqrt{5}}$. Then subtract the result from 496 and write the answer in the grid
6. Determine the length of side x in the triangle giving your answer in the form $a\sqrt{2}\sqrt{5}$ cm. Then multiply the value of a by 129 and write the result in the grid

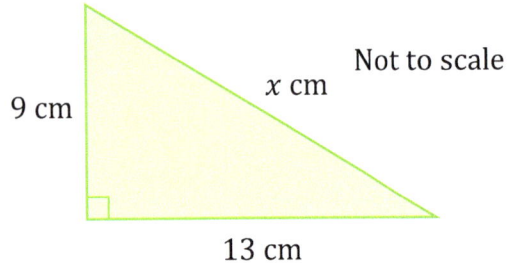

8. Evaluate $(5^7 \div 5^5) - (2 \times 5^0)$
9. What is the value of $25^{2\frac{1}{2}}$?
12. Find the value of $196^{\frac{1}{2}} \times 4^{-\frac{1}{2}} \times 31^2$
15. Simplify $2x^3 y \times 5y^2$ and evaluate the result when $x = 1$ and $y = 3$

Down

1. Express $\frac{2 + \sqrt{8}}{3 - \sqrt{8}}$ in the form $a + b\sqrt{2}$. Then multiply the value of a by 11 and write the result in the grid
2. Evaluate $5 \times (\sqrt{13})^2$
3. Express $\frac{72}{\sqrt{3}}$ in the form $a\sqrt{3}$. Then multiply the value of a by 26 and write the result in the grid
4. Determine the area of the rectangle below giving your answer in the form $(a + b\sqrt{2})$ cm². Then determine the product of values a and b and write the result in the grid

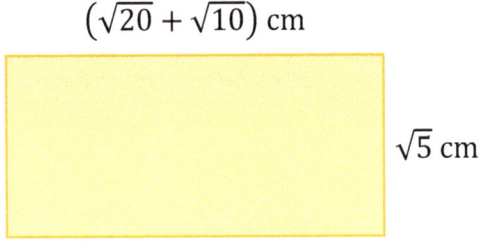

6. Determine the perimeter of the rectangle in clue 4 down giving your answer in the form $2\sqrt{5}(a + \sqrt{b})$ cm. Then multiply the value of a by 21 and write the result in the grid
7. What is 3^{-2} of 486?
8. Simplify $(u^2)^4$ and evaluate the result when $u = 2$

Across continued

No further clues across

Down continued

10. What is the value of $9^2 + 216^{\frac{2}{3}}$?
11. Evaluate $2^7 \times 16^{-\frac{1}{2}}$
13. Calculate $\left(6\frac{1}{4}\right)^{-\frac{1}{2}} \times 190$
14. Simplify $\frac{3x^4y^2 \times 8xy}{4x^3y^2}$ and evaluate the result when $x = 5$ and $y = 0.5$

Indices

Laws of indices

$a^m \times a^n = a^{m+n}$ $a^m \div a^n = a^{m-n}$ $(a^m)^n = a^{m \times n}$ $a^0 = 1$ and $a^1 = a$

$a^{-m} = \frac{1}{a^m}$ $a^{\frac{1}{m}} = \sqrt[m]{a}$ $a^{\frac{m}{n}} = \left(\sqrt[n]{a}\right)^m$ $a^{-\frac{m}{n}} = \frac{1}{\left(\sqrt[n]{a}\right)^m}$

Examples	Solutions
Evaluate $2^3 \times 20^0$	$2^3 \times 20^0 = 8 \times 1 = 8$
Evaluate $4^3 \times 2^{-2}$	$64 \times \frac{1}{2^2} = 64 \times \frac{1}{4} = 16$
Evaluate $144^{\frac{1}{2}} \times 27^{-\frac{2}{3}}$	$\sqrt{144} \times \frac{1}{\left(\sqrt[3]{27}\right)^2} = 12 \times \frac{1}{9} = \frac{4}{3}$
Evaluate $(6^9 \div 6^6) + (3^3)^2$	$6^{9-6} + 3^{3 \times 2} = 6^3 + 3^6 = 216 + 729 = 945$
Simplify $8x^5y \times 3x^2y^2$	$(8 \times 3)x^{5+2}y^{1+2} = 24x^7y^3$

Surds

Rules for surds

$\sqrt{a} \times \sqrt{b} = \sqrt{ab}$ $\left(\sqrt{a}\right)^2 = a$ $\frac{\sqrt{a}}{\sqrt{b}} = \sqrt{\frac{a}{b}}$

Examples	Solutions
Evaluate $\sqrt{7} \times \sqrt{28}$	$\sqrt{7 \times 28} = \sqrt{196} = 14$
Evaluate $\left(\sqrt{11}\right)^2 + \frac{\sqrt{90}}{\sqrt{10}}$	$11 + \sqrt{\frac{90}{10}} = 11 + \sqrt{9} = 11 + 3 = 14$
Simplify $(2 + \sqrt{6})(3 - \sqrt{6})$	$6 - 2\sqrt{6} + 3\sqrt{6} - \sqrt{6}\sqrt{6} = 6 + \sqrt{6} - 6 = \sqrt{6}$
Simplify $\frac{34}{\sqrt{2}}$	$\frac{34}{\sqrt{2}} \times \frac{\sqrt{2}}{\sqrt{2}} = \frac{34\sqrt{2}}{2} = 17\sqrt{2}$
Simplify $\frac{1-\sqrt{3}}{2+\sqrt{3}}$	$\frac{(1-\sqrt{3})(2-\sqrt{3})}{(2+\sqrt{3})(2-\sqrt{3})} = \frac{2 - \sqrt{3} - 2\sqrt{3} + \sqrt{3}\sqrt{3}}{4 - 2\sqrt{3} + 2\sqrt{3} - \sqrt{3}\sqrt{3}} = \frac{2 - 3\sqrt{3} + 3}{4 - 3} = 5 - 3\sqrt{3}$

Crossword 4: Fractions, Decimals and Percentages

Across

1. Put the following fractions in ascending order. Then add the smallest fraction to the largest fraction
$$\frac{7}{8}, \frac{49}{4}, \frac{15}{2}, \frac{12}{8}, \frac{3}{4}, \frac{4}{4}$$
3. What is the value of x in the equivalent fractions $\frac{5}{6} = \frac{45}{x}$?
4. What is the value of $6 \times 4\frac{2}{5} \times 1\frac{2}{3}$?
5. Convert $0.40\dot{5}$ to a fraction in its lowest terms. Then write the denominator value in the grid
7. Work out $\frac{3.6 \times (14.75 - (-19.5))}{0.018}$
9. Convert $0.8\dot{6}\dot{3}$ to a fraction in its lowest terms. Then write the numerator value in the grid
10. Convert $0.\dot{3}\dot{9}$ to a fraction in its lowest terms. Then write the denominator value in the grid
11. Work out $\left(6\frac{3}{10} + 2\frac{4}{5}\right) \div \frac{1}{70}$
13. Reduce £500 by 48%. Write the answer in pounds (£) in the grid
14. The heptagon usually sells for £420 and the octagon usually sells for £700. In a sale there is a third off the price of the heptagon and 15% off the octagon's price. Susan buys both shapes in the sale. How many pounds does Susan pay in total for the two shapes?

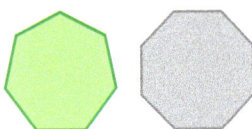

Down

1. Express the following mixed number as an improper fraction in its lowest terms. Then write the numerator value of the improper fraction in the grid
$$14\frac{5}{7}$$
2. There are 876 children in a school. A quarter of the children are in year 6. A third of the children in year 6 are boys. How many girls are in year 6?
3. A quiz team wins $\frac{9}{25}$ of its matches, draws $\frac{1}{8}$ of its matches and loses the rest. If the team plays 1000 matches, how many matches would you expect them to lose?
6. Work out $\frac{0.8 \times 356.5}{\sqrt{0.16}}$
8. The line below is to be increased in length by 36%. What is its new length in millimetres?

6 metres
_____

Not to scale

10. Convert $\frac{41}{125}$ to a decimal and write the three digits after the decimal point in the grid
12. A laptop computer was sold for £553 in a sale that saw 30% off the prices of all items in the store. Write down the usual cost of the laptop (in pounds) outside the sale period

Across continued

15. A square is shown below inside a rectangle of length 72 cm and width 20 cm. The perimeter of the square is 48 cm. What percentage of the rectangle is shaded?

20 cm ▭ Not to scale

72 cm

Down continued

13. The price of the toy cylinder below was recorded in 2006 and 2017. Work out the percentage increase in the cost of the toy

Year	Toy cost
2006	£5.28
2017	£6.60

Fractions and Decimals

Examples	Solutions
Express $6\frac{3}{4}$ as an improper fraction	$6\frac{3}{4} = \frac{(6 \times 4) + 3}{4} = \frac{24 + 3}{4} = \frac{27}{4}$
Calculate $\frac{7}{10} + 3\frac{1}{2}$	$\frac{7}{10} + 3\frac{1}{2} = \frac{7}{10} + \frac{7}{2} = \frac{7}{10} + \left(\frac{7}{2} \times \frac{5}{5}\right) = \frac{7}{10} + \frac{35}{10} = \frac{(7+35)}{10} = \frac{42}{10} = \frac{21}{5} = 4\frac{1}{5}$
Calculate $3\frac{1}{3} \times 2\frac{4}{5}$	$3\frac{1}{3} \times 2\frac{4}{5} = \frac{10}{3} \times \frac{14}{5} = \frac{(10 \times 14)}{(3 \times 5)} = \frac{140}{15} = \frac{28}{3} = 9\frac{1}{3}$
Calculate $2\frac{3}{5} \div \frac{1}{15}$	$2\frac{3}{5} \div \frac{1}{15} = \frac{13}{5} \div \frac{1}{15} = \frac{13}{5} \times \frac{15}{1} = \frac{13}{1} \times \frac{3}{1} = 13 \times 3 = 39$
Calculate $\frac{1.55 + (1.5)^2}{\sqrt{0.64}}$	$\frac{1.55 + (1.5)^2}{\sqrt{0.64}} = \frac{1.55 + 2.25}{0.8} = \frac{3.8}{0.8} = 4.75$
Convert 0.34 to a fraction	$0.34 = \frac{34}{100} = \frac{17}{50}$
Convert $0.\dot{5}$ to a fraction	If $x = 0.555555..$, $10x - x = 5.555555.. - 0.555555.. = 5$. Therefore, $9x = 5$. $x = \frac{5}{9}$
Convert $0.2\dot{1}\dot{8}$ to a fraction	If $x = 0.2181818..$, $1000x - 10x = 218.1818.. - 2.1818.. = 216$. Therefore, $990x = 216$. $x = \frac{216}{990} = \frac{12}{55}$
Convert $\frac{219}{250}$ to a decimal	$\frac{219}{250} \times \frac{4}{4} = \frac{876}{1000} = 0.876$

Percentages

Examples	Solutions
Work out 18% of 500	$\frac{18}{100} \times 500 = 18 \times 5 = 90$
Increase 40 by 5%	$1.05 \times 40 = 42$
Decrease £46 by 20%	$£46 - (0.2 \times £46) = £46 - £9.20 = £36.80$
A number n is increased by 45% to give 87. What is the value of n?	$1.45 \times n = 87$. Therefore, $n = \frac{87}{1.45} = 60$
The capacity of a theatre increases from 250 to 420. What is the percentage increase in capacity?	% increase $= \frac{(\text{new value} - \text{old value})}{\text{old value}} \times 100$ $= \frac{(420 - 250)}{250} \times 100 = \frac{170}{250} \times 100 = 68\%$

Crossword 5: Measures, Approximation and Estimation

Across

2. If there are 534 calories in 100 grams of chocolate and one chocolate bar weighs 45 grams, how many calories are in six identical bars of chocolate? Give your answer to the nearest calorie
4. Round 8.300724 to 3 decimal places. Then multiply the rounded value by 1000
5. Work out the area of the circle below in cm² to 4 significant figures

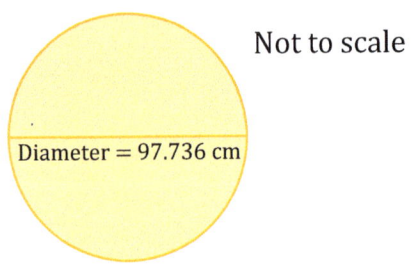

8. Round 0.0078519 to 2 significant figures. Then multiply the rounded value by 10000
11. Estimate $\sqrt{4.69 \times (5.24)^2 + 101.94}$
12. Estimate $\dfrac{8.4 \times 42}{0.47}$
14. Estimate $(87.04 - (2.81)^3) \times 8.85$
15. In the triangle $a = 409.5$ cm and $b = 742.6$ cm (both are given to the nearest mm). Calculate the upper bound for side c and round it to the nearest cm

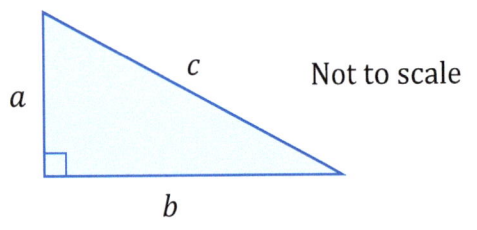

Down

1. If the exchange rate between pounds (£) and Russian rubles is £1 = 75.84 rubles, convert £17.50 to rubles. Give your answer to the nearest ruble
2. An empty cuboid water tank is shown below. Water is about to be poured into the tank at a constant rate of 35 litres every minute. Given that 1 m³ = 1000 litres, in how many minutes will the tank be 90% full of water?

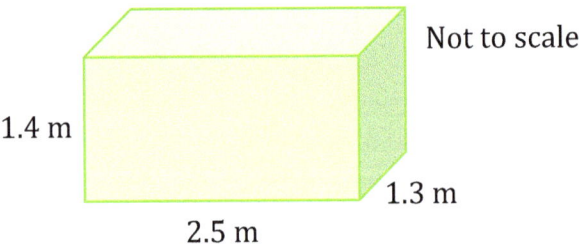

3. Round 409.349 to 2 significant figures
6. Round 58108.09999 to the nearest whole number
7. One atom of silver has an approximate mass of 1.8×10^{-22} grams. Approximately, how many atoms of silver are in 540 grams of silver? Give your answer in standard form of $a \times 10^b$ and write the value of b in the grid
9. If $D = xy$, $x = 55.21$ to 2 decimal places and $y = 180.6$ to 1 decimal place. Calculate the lower bound of D and round it to the nearest whole number
10. A number n when rounded to 1 decimal place is 2.7. Work out the error interval for n in the form $a \leq n < b$. Multiply the value of a by 100 and write the result in the grid

Across continued

No further clues across

Down continued

13. If $T = \frac{x}{y}$, $x = 9$ to 1 significant figure and $y = 0.34$ to 2 significant figures. Calculate the upper bound of T and round it to the nearest whole number

Measures, Rounding and Estimation

Rules when estimating

Estimation is carried out by approximating each value in the calculation to 1 significant figure

Examples	Solutions
If £1 = 1.2 euros, how many pounds is 236 euros? Give your answer to the nearest pound	236 euros = $\frac{236}{1.2}$ = £196.67 = £197 to the nearest pound
A cube tank has a volume of 3.5 m³. The tank is completely full of water. Water is about to be removed from the tank at a constant rate of 50 litres every minute. Given that 1 m³ = 1000 litres, in how many minutes will the tank be empty?	Capacity of full tank = 3.5 × 1000 = 3500 litres. Time until tank is empty = 3500 ÷ 50 = 70 minutes
Round 0.00926703 to 2 significant figures and 2 decimal places	0.0093 to 2 significant figures. 0.01 to 2 decimal places
Round 1075.904 to 3 significant figures and 1 decimal place	1080 to 3 significant figures. 1075.9 to 1 decimal place
Estimate $(8.34)^2 \times 3.74$	Round each value in the calculation to 1 significant figure. $(8.34)^2 \times 3.74 \approx 8^2 \times 4 = 256$
Estimate $\sqrt{103} \div 0.77$	$\sqrt{103} \div 0.77 \approx \sqrt{100} \div 0.8 = 10 \div 0.8 = 12.5$

Upper and Lower Bounds

Upper and lower bound calculations

Calculation	Lower Bound	Upper Bound
$x + y$	$x_{lower} + y_{lower}$	$x_{upper} + y_{upper}$
$x - y$	$x_{lower} - y_{upper}$	$x_{upper} - y_{lower}$
$x \times y$	$x_{lower} \times y_{lower}$	$x_{upper} \times y_{upper}$
$x \div y$	$x_{lower} \div y_{upper}$	$x_{upper} \div y_{lower}$

Examples	Solutions
If $C = x + y$, $x = 11.8$ to 1 decimal place and $y = 75.04$ to 2 decimal places. Calculate the lower bound of C	$C_{lower} = x_{lower} + y_{lower} = 11.75 + 75.035 = 86.785$
If $U = x \div y$, $x = 110$ to 2 significant figures and $y = 2.6$ to 2 significant figures. Calculate the error interval for U	$U_{lower} = x_{lower} \div y_{upper} = 105 \div 2.65 = 39.62..$ $U_{upper} = x_{upper} \div y_{lower} = 115 \div 2.55 = 45.09..$ Error interval: $39.6 \leq U < 45.1$ to 1 decimal place

Crossword 6: Chapter 1 Consolidation Crossword

Across

1. Calculate $-50 \times (-32 + 6) - (-29)$
4. Evaluate $\dfrac{76 \times (3-5)^2}{12 - (\sqrt{400} \times 0.5)}$
7. What is the area of the symmetrical trapezium below in square metres? Give your answer as an ordinary number

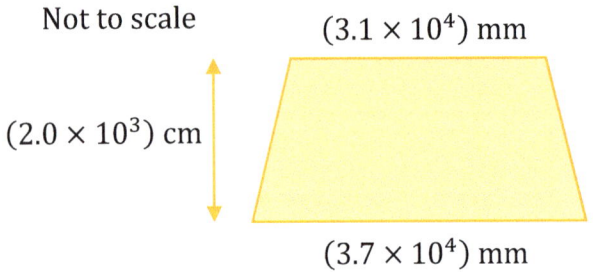

Not to scale (3.1×10^4) mm

(2.0×10^3) cm

(3.7×10^4) mm

8. Sum of all the factors of 102
9. Highest common factor of 75 and 135
12. Determine the area of the square below, giving your answer in the form $(a + b\sqrt{5})$ m². Then multiply the value of b by 20 and write the result in the grid

$(2 + \sqrt{5})$ m

Not to scale

Down

2. The total annual revenue made from subscriptions to a magazine is £20940. £16140 is from adult subsriptions and the remainder is from child subscriptions. An annual child subscription is £15. How many child subsriptions are there?
3. What is the 123rd multiple of 75?
4. Write 208 as the product of its prime factors. Then multiply the largest prime factor of 208 by 120 and write the result in the grid
5. Express $\sqrt{1053} + \dfrac{156}{\sqrt{52}}$ in the form $a\sqrt{13}$. Then multiply the value of a by 1800 and write the result in the grid
6. Two cogs are shown below. Cog A has 10 teeth and cog B has 12 teeth. The cogs begin to slowly rotate. It takes 4.5 minutes for cog A to complete a whole revolution. How many seconds will it take both cogs to first return to the same positions at the same time?

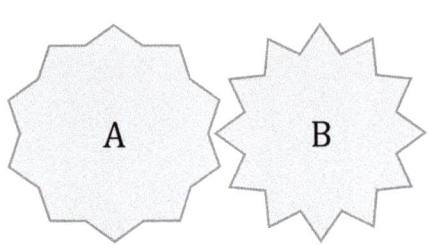

Across continued

14. Work out $\dfrac{120 \times (219.67 + 37.05)}{1.2}$

15. What is the area of the triangle below in square centimetres?

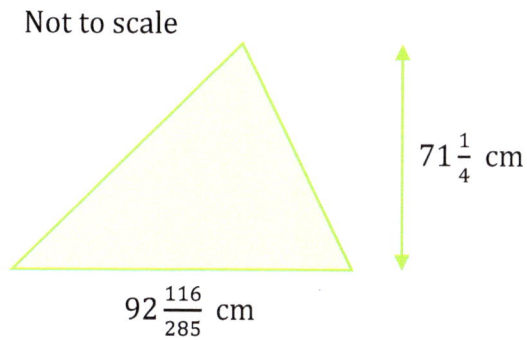

Not to scale

$71\tfrac{1}{4}$ cm

$92\tfrac{116}{285}$ cm

17. A stamp collection increased in size from 800 to 1192. By what percentage did the stamp collection grow?

19. Convert $0.3\dot{8}$ to a fraction in its lowest terms. Then write the denominator value in the grid

21. A container had 7 litres of water in it. Two-fifths of the water was drunk by Donna. 87% of the water that remained was given to Anna and the rest was given to Palin. How many millilitres of water did Palin receive?

22. Determine the volume of the cylinder below in cm³ to 2 significant figures

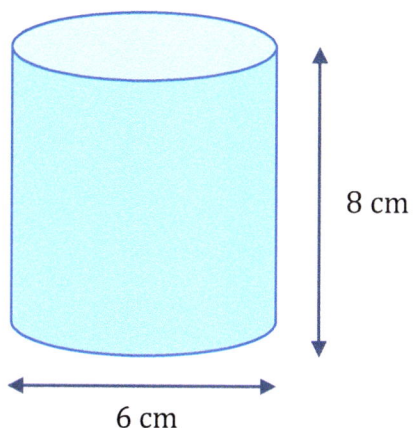

Not to scale

8 cm

6 cm

Down continued

10. A shop stocks 18 different drinks, 5 different packs of biscuits and 4 different packs of chewing gum. A customer walks into the shop and chooses one of:
    a) a pack of biscuits and a drink,
    b) a drink and a pack of chewing gum,
    c) a drink, pack of biscuits and pack of chewing gum.

    How many ways are there for the customer to make their selection?

11. Simplify $11 \times (27x^9)^{\tfrac{1}{3}} \div x^{\tfrac{5}{2}}$ and evaluate the result when $x = 4$

12. Work out $\left(12\tfrac{2}{5} - 4\tfrac{4}{25}\right) \times 100$

13. Evaluate $7^0 \times 7^1 + 5^4 \times 5^{-2}$

15. Determine the radius of the circle in metres as a decimal. Then write the radius in millimetres in the grid

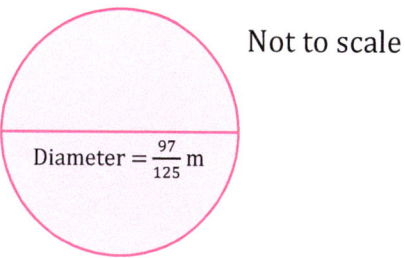

Not to scale

Diameter $= \dfrac{97}{125}$ m

16. Reduce 1125 by 16%

18. Estimate $(1.67 + 41.1 + (7.32)^2) \times \sqrt[3]{1015}$

20. In the parallelogram $a = 22.7$ cm and $b = 18.4$ cm (both are given to the nearest mm). Calculate the lower bound for the perimeter of the parallelogram in centimetres

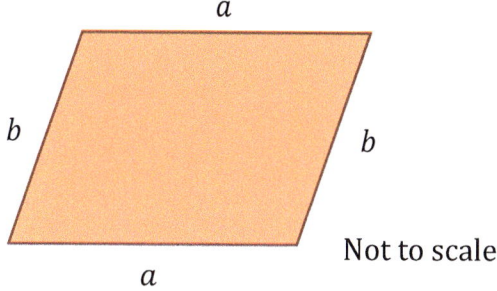

Not to scale

Chapter 2
Algebra

Crossword 7: Algebraic Methods

Note: assume that values a, b and c are always integers in this crossword

Across

1. Simplify $8p + 2p \times 3p - p + 5p$ into the form $ap(p+b)$. What is the product of values a and b?
3. Simplify $(-3x)^2 + (12x - (-2x)) \times 2x$ fully and from the simplified expression write the coefficient of x^2 in the grid
6. A cuboid is shown below along with its dimensions. Form an expression for the volume of the cuboid. Expand and fully simplify the expression. From the expanded expression, multiply the coefficient of the x^2 term by 93 and write the result in the grid

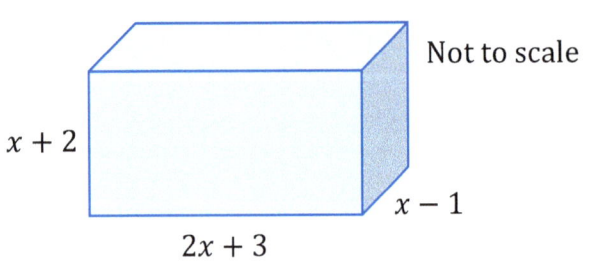

Not to scale

8. Expand $4(t-15) + 8(3t+60)$ and simplify the result into the form $at+b$. What is the value of b?
10. Factorise $54x^2 - 6$ fully into the form $a(bx+1)(bx-1)$. What is the result of subtracting the value of b from 718?
11. Factorise $y^2 + 24y + 44$ fully into the form $(y+a)(y+b)$ where $b > a$. What is the value of b?
12. Simplify $\frac{4x+12}{x^2+10x+21} \div \frac{x-7}{x^3-49x}$ into the form ax. Then multiply the value of a by 490

Down

2. If $Z = (y^2 - 8xy) \div 6x$, what is the value of Z when $x = 0.25$ and $y = 20$?
4. If $P = 3w\sqrt{v} + 50x$, what is the value of P when $v = 144$, $w = 200$ and $x = 3$?
5. The rectangular garden below is made up of a section of grass and a section of pavement. Form an expression for the area of the garden. Expand and fully simplify the expression. From the simplified expression, write the coefficient of the x term in the grid

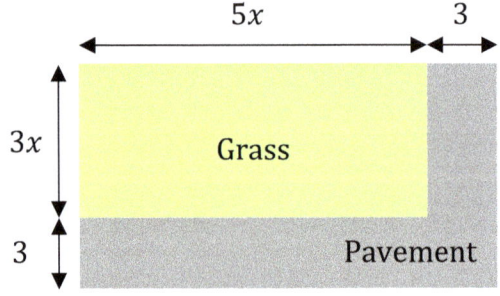

Not to scale

7. Expand $(m-22)(m-26)$ fully and simplify the result into the form $m^2 + am + b$. What is the value of b?
9. Expand $(2x-5)^2 + 264$ fully and simplify the result into the form $ax^2 + bx + c$. What is the value of c?
11. Factorise $3y^2 - 28y - 20$ fully into the form $(3y+a)(y-b)$. What is the value of $10a$?
12. Simplify $\frac{6}{x+2} - \frac{3}{(x+2)^2}$ into the form $\frac{a(bx+c)}{(x+2)^2}$. Then add the value of c to 98
13. Simplify $\frac{1}{x} + \frac{20}{x+5}$ into the form $\frac{ax+b}{x(x+5)}$. Then multiply the value of a by 31

Across continued

15. Make x the subject of $y + 2 = 2x + 9$. What is the value of x when $y = 613$?
17. Make y the subject of $\frac{1}{x} = \frac{4}{y^2}$. What is the positive value of y when $x = 8649$?

Down continued

14. Make t the subject of $x = \frac{t}{2} - 3x$. What is the value of t when $x = 5$?
15. Make x the subject of $\sqrt{2x(y-1)} = 15 - y$. What is the value of x when $y = 3$?
16. Make m the subject of $m - 2 = \frac{m-16}{n}$. What is the value of m when $n = 0.5$?

Algebraic Methods

Rules

$mn = m \times n$ $\qquad m^2 = m \times m \qquad 4m = m + m + m + m$

$\frac{m}{n} = m \div n \qquad$ Difference of two squares: $m^2 - n^2 = (m+n)(m-n)$

Examples	Solutions
Simplify $3p + 6p \times 4p - 2p$	$3p + 6p \times 4p - 2p = 3p + 24p^2 - 2p = 24p^2 + p = p(24p + 1)$
If $Q = (5xy - x^2) \div \sqrt{8x + 1}$, what is the value of Q when $x = 6$ and $y = 4$?	$Q = (5 \times 6 \times 4 - (6)^2) \div \sqrt{(8 \times 6) + 1} = 84 \div 7 = 12$
Expand and simplify $(2m - 5)(m + 4)$	$(2m - 5)(m + 4) = 2m^2 + 8m - 5m - 20 = 2m^2 + 3m - 20$
Expand and simplify $(3m - 1)(m + 2)(m + 3)$	$(3m^2 + 5m - 2)(m + 3) =$ $m(3m^2 + 5m - 2) + 3(3m^2 + 5m - 2) =$ $3m^3 + 5m^2 - 2m + 9m^2 + 15m - 6 = 3m^3 + 14m^2 + 13m - 6$
Factorise $2y^2 - 8y - 10$	$2y^2 - 8y - 10 = (2y + 2)(y - 5)$
Simplify $\frac{1}{x} + \frac{2}{x-3}$	$\frac{1}{x} \times \frac{x-3}{x-3} + \frac{2}{x-3} \times \frac{x}{x} = \frac{x - 3 + 2x}{x(x-3)} = \frac{3x - 3}{x(x-3)} = \frac{3(x-1)}{x(x-3)}$
Simplify $\frac{x+3}{x^2+5x+6} \div \frac{2(x-2)}{x^3-4x}$	$\frac{x+3}{(x+2)(x+3)} \times \frac{x(x^2-4)}{2(x-2)} = \frac{1}{x+2} \times \frac{x(x+2)(x-2)}{2(x-2)} = \frac{x}{2}$

Changing the Subject of a Formula

Examples	Solutions
Make x the subject of $6y + 2x = cx + 5$	$2x - cx = 5 - 6y$. Therefore, $x(2 - c) = 5 - 6y \Rightarrow x = \frac{5 - 6y}{2 - c}$
Make t the subject of $x = \frac{t^2}{6} - 5x$	Multiply throughout by 6. $6x = t^2 - 30x \Rightarrow t^2 = 6x + 30x$. Therefore, $t^2 = 36x$. $t = \pm\sqrt{36x} = \pm 6\sqrt{x}$
Make x the subject of $a(x - 2) = b(3 + 2x)$	$ax - 2a = 3b + 2bx \Rightarrow ax - 2bx = 3b + 2a$. Therefore, $x(a - 2b) = 3b + 2a \Rightarrow x = \frac{3b + 2a}{a - 2b}$

Crossword 8: Linear Equations and Inequalities

Across

1. Solve the equation $2(x - 200) = 252$
3. Solve $3x - 57 = 2x + 65$
5. Solve $5^{y-38} = 125$
7. Solve $2^{z-7} = 16$
9. Billy, Kimberly and Alpa each have sticker collections. Billy has twice as many stickers as Alpa. Alpa has 124 fewer stickers than Kimberly. Altogether they have 992 stickers between the three of them. How many stickers does Alpa have?
10. Largest integer that satisfies $x - 500 < 400$
11. What is the size of angle y in the rhombus?

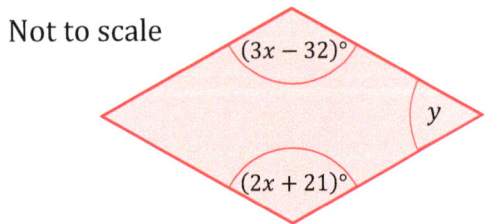

13. Smallest integer that satisfies the inequality represented on the number line below

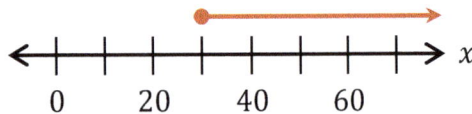

14. Smallest integer that satisfies $7x - 150 > 119 + 3x$
17. Largest integer that satisfies $5x + 1 < 552$
18. Solve the simultaneous equations and write the product of values x and y in the grid

$$5x - 3y = -47$$
$$2x + 7y = 383$$

Down

1. Solve the equation $2x + 16 = 798$
2. Solve $\frac{2(2x - 50)}{6} = 26$
4. Solve $\frac{x}{5} - 225 = 310$
6. A kite and a square are shown below. The perimeters of the shapes are equal. All measurements are in centimetres. What is the area of the square in square millimetres?

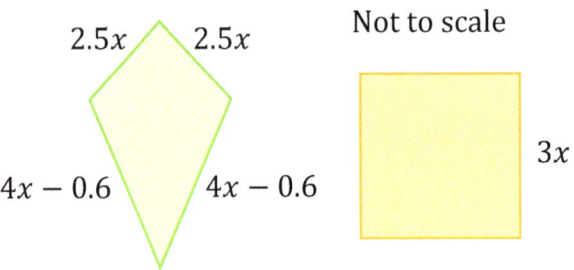

8. A function is represented by the following number machine. The output of the machine is 300. What is the input?

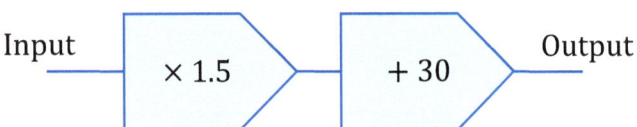

12. n is an integer with $7200 \leq 4n < 7207$. What is the sum of all the possible values of n?
13. Solve the simultaneous equations and write the value of x in the grid

$$2x - 6y = 428$$
$$x + 2y = 389$$

Across continued

No further clues across

Down continued

15. Solve the simultaneous equations and write the product of values x and y in the grid

$$-3x + 8y = -62$$
$$2x - 9y = -10$$

16. Solve the simultaneous equations and write the value of y in the grid

$$4x + y = 30$$
$$y = 2x$$

Linear Equations

Examples	Solutions
Solve $3x + 1 = 7 + x$	$3x + 1 = 7 + x \Rightarrow 3x - x = 7 - 1 \Rightarrow 2x = 6 \Rightarrow x = 3$
Solve $3^{2y-1} = 27$	Make the bases the same. Therefore, $3^{2y-1} = 3^3$. Equate powers. $2y - 1 = 3 \Rightarrow 2y = 3 + 1 \Rightarrow 2y = 4 \Rightarrow y = 2$
Solve the simultaneous equations by the elimination method $5x + 2y = 9$ $3x - 5y = -7$	**Solution by elimination method** Equation 1: $5x + 2y = 9$ and equation 2: $3x - 5y = -7$. Multiply equation 1 by 5 and equation 2 by 2. Equation 3: $25x + 10y = 45$ and equation 4: $6x - 10y = -14$. Add equations 3 and 4 to give: $31x = 31 \Rightarrow \boxed{x = 1}$. Substitute $x = 1$ into equation 1 to give: $5(1) + 2y = 9 \Rightarrow 2y = 9 - 5 \Rightarrow 2y = 4 \Rightarrow \boxed{y = 2}$
Solve the simultaneous equations by the substitution method $3x - y = 5$ $x + y = 7$	**Solution by substitution method** Equation 1: $3x - y = 5$ and equation 2: $x + y = 7$. From equation 2, $y = 7 - x$. Substitute $y = 7 - x$ into equation 1: $3x - (7 - x) = 5 \Rightarrow 3x - 7 + x = 5 \Rightarrow 4x = 5 + 7 \Rightarrow 4x = 12 \Rightarrow \boxed{x = 3}$. $y = 7 - x = 7 - 3 \Rightarrow \boxed{y = 4}$

Linear Inequalities

Examples	Solutions
Solve $2x - 1 > 3 + x$	$2x - 1 > 3 + x \Rightarrow 2x - x > 3 + 1 \Rightarrow x > 4$. The number line below shows this solution. The hollow circle on the end of the line above the 4 indicates that the solution does not include the number 4. The smallest integer that satisfies this inequality is 5
Solve $16 \leq 2n < 25$, given n is an integer	$16 \leq 2n < 25 \Rightarrow 16 \div 2 \leq n < 25 \div 2 \Rightarrow 8 \leq n < 12.5$. The number line below shows this solution. The filled in circle on the end of the line above the 8 indicates that 8 is included in the solution. Therefore, n can take the values: 8, 9, 10, 11, 12

Crossword 9: Straight Line Graphs

Across

1. Write down the gradient for the straight line with equation $y = 15x + 11$
2. Four graphs are shown below with numbers written underneath them. Which graph is a sketch of $y = 2x - 1$? Write the number under the correct graph in the grid

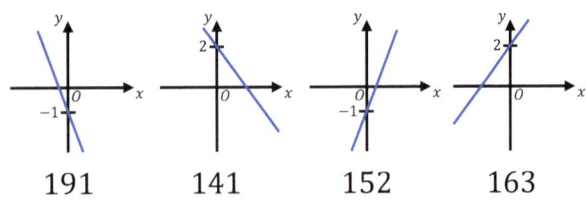

191   141   152   163

4. Find the y-intercept for a straight line which passes through $(5, 5)$ and has gradient -7
5. Find the equation of the straight line which passes through $(6, -7)$ and $(-2, 5)$. Point $P(-152, k)$ also lies on the line. Work out k
7. y-intercept of the straight line which passes through $(3, 250)$ and is parallel to $y = 15x + 5$
9. Straight line CD has equation $y = 32x + 42$. Straight line AB is parallel to CD. What is the gradient of AB?
10. What are the midpoint coordinates of line AB below? Write the x-coordinate of the midpoint coordinates in the grid

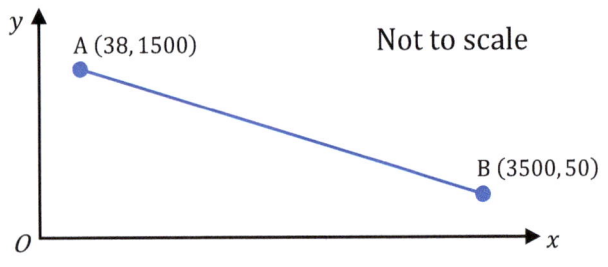

Down

1. Write down the y-intercept for the straight line with equation $y = 103x + 142$
2. Write down the gradient for the straight line with equation $2y - 20x = 22$
3. A straight line has equation $y = 0.5x - 6$. Point $Q(552, k)$ lies on the line. Work out k
4. Draw the graph of equation $y = 5 + 0.25x$ on the grid below. Point $Z(k, 15)$ lies on the line. Use the graph to work out k

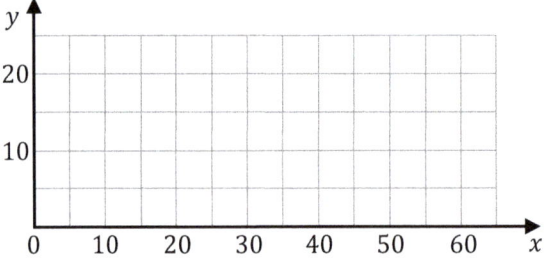

6. y-intercept of the straight line which passes through $(-129, 0)$ and $(10, 417)$
7. Find the gradient for the straight line which passes through $(-1, -53)$ and has y-intercept -31
8. Straight line CD has equation $y = -0.02x + 40$. Line AB is perpendicular to CD. What is the gradient of AB?
9. At which x-coordinate does the line with equation $y = 2x - 782$ cross the x-axis?
10. A straight line with gradient 30 passes through points $(1, 3)$ and $(5, k)$. What is the value of k?
11. Write down the y-intercept for the straight line with equation $6(y - 3x) = 90$

Across continued

12. y-intercept of the straight line which passes through $(160, -128)$ and is perpendicular to $y = \frac{1}{8}x + 35$
15. Shade the region satisfying the inequalities $x \geq 10$, $y \geq 0$ and $y \leq -\frac{2}{3}x + \frac{80}{3}$. What is the area of the shaded region?

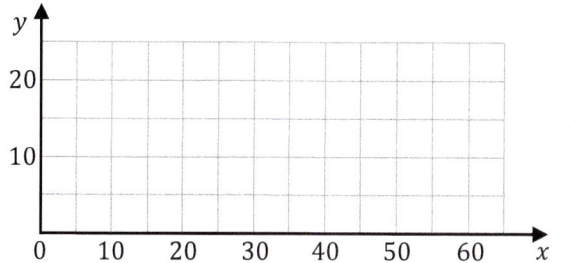

Down continued

13. Determine the midpoint coordinates of the line with end point coordinates $(6, 9)$ and $(32, 27)$. Write the y-coordinate of the midpoint coordinates in the grid
14. The diagram below shows a line from the origin O to point G. The gradient of the line is 3 and the length of the line is $\sqrt{810}$. What is the y-coordinate of point G?

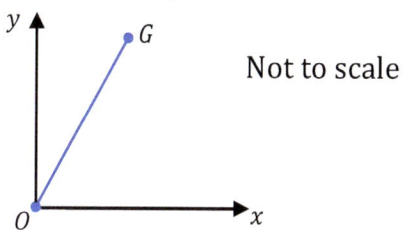

Not to scale

Straight Line Graphs

Equation of straight line: $y = mx + c$

m is the gradient of the line. Positive gradients slant right /. Negative gradients slant left \

The gradient between two points $A\ (x_1, y_1)$ and $B\ (x_2, y_2)$ is given by $m = \frac{\text{change in } y}{\text{change in } x} = \frac{y_2 - y_1}{x_2 - x_1}$

c is the y-intercept, which is the place where the line crosses the y-axis when $x = 0$

Parallel lines have the same gradient. If lines 1 and 2 are perpendicular $m_{\text{line 2}} = -\frac{1}{m_{\text{line 1}}}$

The midpoint coordinates of the line between $A\ (x_1, y_1)$ and $B\ (x_2, y_2)$ are given by $\left(\frac{x_1 + x_2}{2}, \frac{y_1 + y_2}{2}\right)$

Examples	Solutions
Write down the gradient and y-intercept for the straight line with equation $3y + 24x = 18$	$3y = -24x + 18 \Rightarrow y = -8x + 6$. This is now in the form $y = mx + c$ where the gradient $m = -8$ and y-intercept $c = 6$
Find the equation of the straight line which passes through $(2, -3)$ and $(4, 5)$	$m = \frac{y_2 - y_1}{x_2 - x_1} = \frac{5 - -3}{4 - 2} = \frac{8}{2} = 4$. $y = 4x + c, c = y - 4x$. $(4, 5) \rightarrow c = 5 - 4(4) \Rightarrow c = -11$. $y = 4x - 11$
Find the equation of the line which passes through $(-2, 0)$ and is parallel to $y = 2x + 10$	Parallel lines have the same gradient. Therefore, equation of parallel line is $y = 2x + c, c = y - 2x$. $(-2, 0) \rightarrow c = 0 - 2(-2) \Rightarrow c = 4$. $y = 2x + 4$
Find the equation of the line which passes through $(1, 3)$ and is perpendicular to $y = \frac{1}{5}x - 2$	$m_{\text{line 2}} = -\frac{1}{m_{\text{line 1}}} = -\frac{1}{1/5} = -5$. Equation of perpendicular line is $y = -5x + c, c = y + 5x$. $(1, 3) \rightarrow c = 3 + 5(1) \Rightarrow c = 8$. $y = -5x + 8$
Determine the midpoint coordinates of the line with end point coordinates $(-3, 0)$ and $(7, 6)$	$\left(\frac{x_1 + x_2}{2}, \frac{y_1 + y_2}{2}\right) = \left(\frac{-3 + 7}{2}, \frac{0 + 6}{2}\right) = \left(\frac{4}{2}, \frac{6}{2}\right) = (2, 3)$
Shade the region satisfying the inequalities $1 \leq x \leq 4$, $y \geq 0$ and $y \leq x + 1$	

Crossword 10: Quadratic Equations and Inequalities

Across

1. Solve $x^2 - 13x + 22 = 0$ by factorisation and write the largest solution in the grid
2. Solve $x^2 + 6x + 4 = 0$ by completing the square. Express the solution in the form $a \pm \sqrt{b}$. Add 126 to the value of b and write the result in the grid
4. Solve $x^2 - 28x + 3 = 0$. What is the largest solution to the nearest whole number?
5. Solve $-2x^2 + 90x + 45 = 0$. Give the largest solution to the nearest whole number
6. On the graph below determine the largest solution for the quadratic when $y = 0$

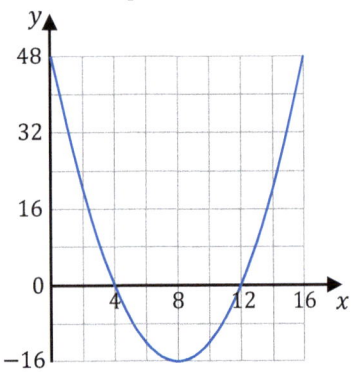

8. For the graph in clue 6 across, what is the result of multiplying 160 by the smallest solution to the quadratic when $y = 0$?
10. Determine the equation of the curve in clue 6 across in the form $y = x^2 + bx + c$. Point $W(-1, k)$ lies on the curve. Work out k
11. What are the coordinates of the turning point on the quadratic in clue 6 across? Multiply the x-coordinate of the turning point by 3 and write the result in the grid

Down

1. Solve $4x^2 - 13x - 6 = 3x(x - 4)$. Multiply the largest solution by 47 and write the result in the grid
2. Write $2x^2 - 8x + 9 = 0$ in the form $a(x - b)^2 + c = 0$. Subtract the value of c from 187 and write the result in the grid
3. Rectangle ABCD has the same area as triangle PQR. All sides are measured in centimetres. What is the length of side QR on the triangle in millimetres?

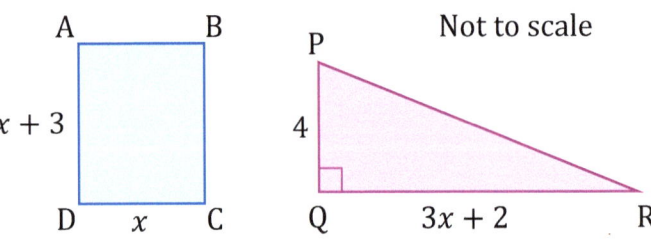

7. Write $-x^2 + 20x + 164$ in the form $-a(x - b)^2 + c$. Hence, write down the y-coordinate of the turning point of the graph $y = -x^2 + 20x + 164$
9. Write $3x^2 + 18x + 15$ in the form $a(x + b)^2 - c$. Hence, add 4792 to the value of the y-coordinate of the turning point of the graph $y = 3x^2 + 18x + 15$ and write the result in the grid
11. What is the result of squaring the y-coordinate of the turning point on the graph $y = 2x^2 + 16x + 17$?
13. Multiply 450 by the largest positive integer which satisfies $x^2 + 8x - 33 < 0$

Across continued

12. Multiply 91 by the smallest positive integer which satisfies $x^2 > 4(x + 8)$
14. Multiply 20 by the largest positive integer which satisfies $x^2 - 12x + 27 \leq 0$
15. Solve the simultaneous equations below. Add 551 to the largest solution for y and write the result in the grid

$$y + 4x = 2$$
$$y - x^2 = 5$$

16. Solve the simultaneous equations below. Write the largest solution for y in the grid

$$y^2 + x^2 = 100$$
$$y + x = 10$$

Down continued

14. Two function machines are shown below. The input to both function machines is x^2. Determine the sum of all integer values of x for which the output of machine 1 is less than the output of machine 2

Function machine 1

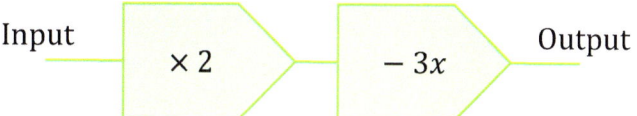

Function machine 2

Quadratic Equations and Inequalities

A quadratic equation takes the form $y = ax^2 + bx + c$.

The following formula will always solve $ax^2 + bx + c = 0$:

Turning point occurs at $x = -\frac{b}{2a}$

Quadratic formula $x = \frac{-b \pm \sqrt{b^2 - 4ac}}{2a}$

Examples	Solutions
Solve $x^2 + 6x - 7 = 0$ by factorisation	$x^2 + 6x - 7 = 0 \Rightarrow (x + 7)(x - 1) = 0 \Rightarrow x + 7 = 0$ or $x - 1 = 0$. Therefore, $x = -7$ or $x = 1$. These are also known as the roots
Solve $-2x^2 + 5x + 4 = 0$ using the quadratic formula	$x = \frac{-b \pm \sqrt{b^2 - 4ac}}{2a} = \frac{-5 \pm \sqrt{(5)^2 - 4(-2)(4)}}{2(-2)} = \frac{-5 \pm \sqrt{57}}{-4} = -0.64$ or 3.14
Solve $2x^2 + 4x - 3 = 0$ by completing the square	**Step 1:** From the x^2 and x terms, form $p(x^2 + qx)$. $$2x^2 + 4x = 2(x^2 + 2x)$$ **Step 2:** Write $p(x^2 + qx) = p\left(x + \frac{q}{2}\right)^2$ and expand. $$2(x^2 + 2x) = 2\left(x + \frac{2}{2}\right)^2 = 2(x + 1)^2 = 2x^2 + 4x + 2$$ **Step 3:** Compare result from step 2 with original and adjust. $$2x^2 + 4x - 3 = 2x^2 + 4x + 2 - 5 = 2(x + 1)^2 - 5 = 0$$ **Step 4:** Solve the equation. $$2(x + 1)^2 - 5 = 0 \Rightarrow (x + 1)^2 = \frac{5}{2} \Rightarrow x = -1 \pm \sqrt{\frac{5}{2}}$$
Find the turning point of $y = 2x^2 + 4x - 3$	$x = -\frac{b}{2a} = -\frac{4}{2(2)} = -1$. $y = 2(-1)^2 + 4(-1) - 3 = -5$. Therefore, the turning point is at coordinates $(-1, -5)$
Solve the simultaneous equations $4x - y = 4$, $x^2 + y = 1$	From equation 1: $y = 4x - 4$. Substitute into equation 2: $x^2 + (4x - 4) = 1 \Rightarrow x^2 + 4x - 5 = 0 \Rightarrow (x + 5)(x - 1) = 0$. $x = -5, y = 4(-5) - 4 = -24$ and $x = 1, y = 4(1) - 4 = 0$
Solve $x^2 + 2x - 15 < 0$	$x^2 + 2x - 15 < 0 \Rightarrow (x + 5)(x - 3) < 0$. The graph of this function will be less than 0 for $-5 < x < 3$
Solve $x^2 - 6x + 8 \geq 0$	$x^2 - 6x + 8 \geq 0 \Rightarrow (x - 2)(x - 4) \geq 0$. The graph of this function will be greater than or equal to 0 for $x \leq 2$ and $x \geq 4$

Crossword 11: Functions and Transformations

Across

1. The function f is given by $f(x) = 10x + 3$. Find the value of $f(12)$
3. The function g is given by $g(x) = \frac{1}{4}x + 2$. Find the value of $g^{-1}(7)$
4. If $f(x) = 3 - \sqrt{x}$ and $g(x) = 3x^2 + 7$, find $gf(4)$
5. If $f(x) = \frac{x^2 + 6}{3}$ and $g(x) = 7 + 2x$, find $gf(-30)$
6. If $f(x) = kx + 2$ and $f(8) = 18$, what is the value of $g(292)$ if $g(x) = k(x - 1)$?
8. If $f(x) = x + 2$, solve $f^{-1}(p) = 85$ for p
11. The graph of $f(x) = \sin x°$ is shown below. Sketch $-f(x)$ on the same grid and determine the sum of all x values in $0° \leq x \leq 720°$ for which $-f(x) = -1$

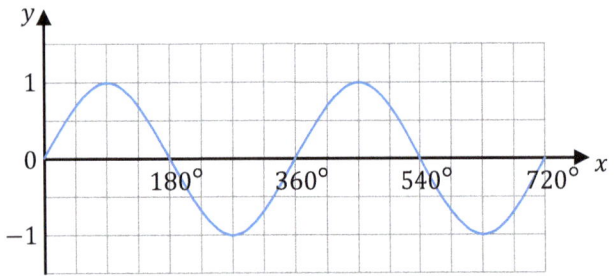

12. If $f(x) = x^2 - 3x - 4$, at what value does the graph of $y = f(x) + 529$ intersect the y-axis?
13. If $f(x) = x^3$, what is the value of $f(-x)$ when $x = -6$?
14. If $f(x) = \cos x°$, what is the value of x in the interval $0° \leq x \leq 90°$ for which $f(2x) = 0$?

Down

1. The function f is given by $f(x) = 3(5 - 2x)$. Find the value of $ff(5)$
2. The function g is given by $g(x) = 6x + 1$. Find the value of $g^{-1}(7) + g(60)$
3. $f(x) = x + p$ and $g(x) = 2 + q + qx$ where p and q are integers. If $fg(x) = 223 + 3x$, what is the value of p?
7. Four graphs are shown below with numbers written underneath them. Which graph is a sketch of $f(x) = \frac{1}{x}$? Write the number under the correct graph in the grid

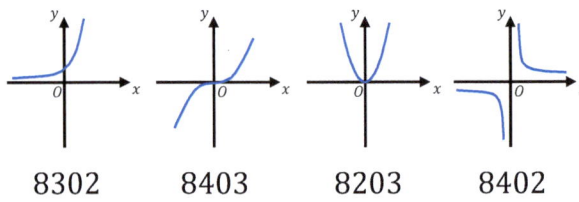

8302   8403   8203   8402

9. Four graphs are shown below with numbers written underneath them. Which graph is a sketch of $f(x) = 2^{-x}$? Write the number under the correct graph in the grid

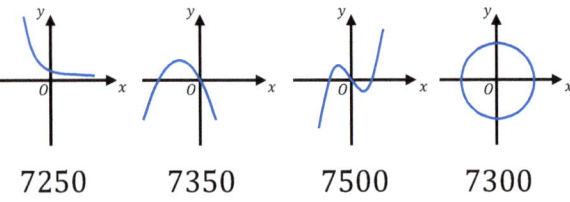

7250   7350   7500   7300

10. If $f(x) = -x^3 + 4x$, what is the sum of all values of x for which $f(x - 521) = 0$?

Across continued

15. The diagram below shows the circle with equation $x^2 + y^2 = 29$. Work out the equation of the tangent to the circle at point $P(-2, 5)$. Using the equation of the tangent, what is the value of y when $x = 68$?

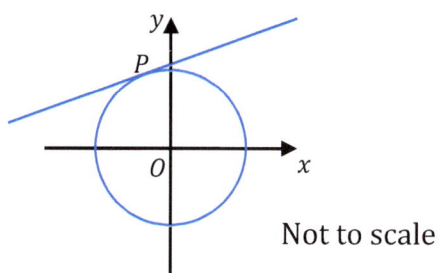

Not to scale

Down continued

11. The diagram below shows the circle with equation $x^2 + y^2 = 101$. Point $P(10, k)$, lies on the circle. Work out the equation of the tangent to the circle at point P. Using the equation of the tangent, what is the value of y when $x = -49.3$?

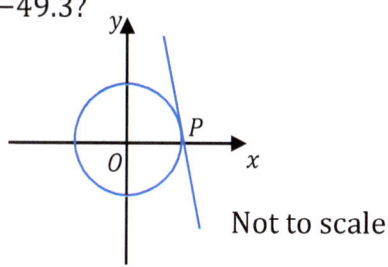

Not to scale

Functions and Transformations

Examples	Solutions
If $f(x) = x - 2$ and $g(x) = 2x^2 + 1$, determine $gf(5)$	$gf(x) = 2(x-2)^2 + 1 = 2(x^2 - 4x + 4) + 1 = 2x^2 - 8x + 9$. $gf(5) = 2(5)^2 - 8(5) + 9 = 50 - 40 + 9 = 19$
If $f(x) = \frac{2x - 1}{3}$, work out $f^{-1}(3)$	Let $f(x) = x$ and $x = f^{-1}(x)$. Therefore, $x = \frac{2f^{-1}(x) - 1}{3}$. $2f^{-1}(x) = 3x + 1 \Rightarrow f^{-1}(x) = \frac{3x + 1}{2} \Rightarrow f^{-1}(3) = \frac{3(3) + 1}{2} = 5$
$f(x) = x^2 - 4x + 3$ is shown by the red line on both graphs. On the left graph $f(-x)$ is in purple and on the right graph $f(x - 2)$ is in purple	$f(-x)$ is a reflection in the y-axis / $f(x - 2)$ moves the graph 2 units right
$f(x) = \cos x°$ is shown by the red line on both graphs. On the left graph $-f(x)$ is in purple. On the right graph $f(2x)$ is in purple	$-f(x)$ is a reflection in the x-axis / For $f(2x)$ the x-values are halved

Circles and Tangents

Equation of circle with centre $(0, 0)$: $x^2 + y^2 = r^2$ where r is the radius of the circle.

The gradient of a tangent (T) to the circle is perpendicular to the gradient of the radius: $m_T = -\frac{1}{m_r}$

Examples	Solutions
Point $P(k, 4)$ lies on the circle with equation $x^2 + y^2 = 25$. What is the equation of the tangent to the circle at point P?	Point $P(k, 4) \Rightarrow k^2 = 25 - 4^2 \Rightarrow k = 3$. $P(3, 4)$. Gradient (m_r) of radius $OP = \frac{4}{3}$. Gradient of tangent (m_T) $= -\frac{1}{m_r} = -\frac{1}{4/3} = -\frac{3}{4}$. Tangent: $y = -\frac{3}{4}x + c$. Substitute in $(3, 4) \Rightarrow$ $4 = -\frac{3}{4}(3) + c \Rightarrow c = \frac{25}{4}$. $\boxed{y = -\frac{3}{4}x + \frac{25}{4}}$

Crossword 12: Iterations, Sequences and Real-Life Graphs

Across

2. An iterative process is given by $x_{n+1} = \sqrt[3]{24 - 2x_n}$ and $x_0 = 2$. Calculate x_3 rounded to 1 decimal place. Multiply the rounded solution by 10
4. If $x_{n+1} = \sqrt{16x_n - 5}$ and $x_0 = 15$, find x_1 in the form $\sqrt{a}\sqrt{5}$. What is the value of a?
5. If $x_{n+1} = \sqrt{7x_n - 3}$ and $x_0 = 6$, find the solution to 2 significant figures. Multiply the rounded solution by 10
7. What is the next term in the sequence 23, 46, 92, 184?
8. What is the next term in the sequence 256, 225, 196, 169?
9. The first four terms of a Fibonacci sequence are $p, q, p+q, p+2q$. If the 4th term is 20 and the 6th term is 53, what is the 7th term?
11. A sequence is given by $U_{n+1} = \frac{(U_n)^2 + U_n}{2}$. Given $U_1 = 2$, calculate $U_4 - U_3$
12. Find the position-to-term formula U_n for the quadratic sequence $-27, -20, -9, 6, 25$. Hence, find the next term of the sequence
15. The first four terms in a sequence are $\sqrt{2}, 2, 2\sqrt{2}, 4$. What is the 10th term?
16. The distance-time graph is for a car journey. How many seconds was the car stationary?

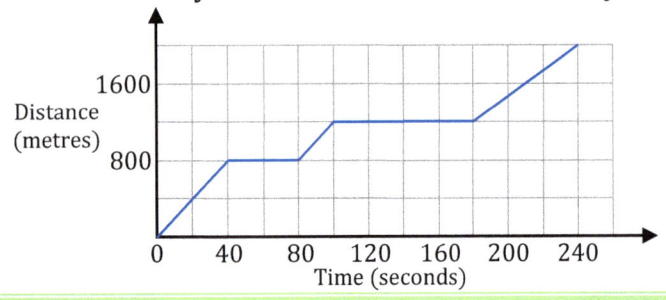

Down

1. Starting with $x_0 = 0$, use the iteration formula $x_{n+1} = \frac{1}{2} - \frac{(x_n)^3}{2}$ to calculate x_2 in fractional format in its lowest terms. Write the denominator value in the grid
3. The number of ice creams sold in t hours is x_t where $x_0 = 5100$ and $x_{t+1} = 1.2x_t$. Determine x_2
4. If $x_{n+1} = \frac{1}{2} - \frac{(x_n)^3}{10}$ and $x_0 = 0.5$, find the solution to 3 decimal places. Multiply the rounded solution by 1000
6. The first five terms in an arithmetic sequence are 8, 11, 14, 17, 20. Find an expression, in terms of n, for the nth term of the sequence and use it to find the 170th term of the sequence
10. The first four terms in an arithmetic sequence are 4, 11, 18, 25. What is the 10th term of the sequence?
11. The nth term of a sequence is $4^n + 4^{n-2}$. What is the sum of the 3rd and 5th terms of the sequence?
13. The speed-time graph for a train journey is shown below. Subtract the total distance travelled by the train from 10202 metres. Give your answer in metres

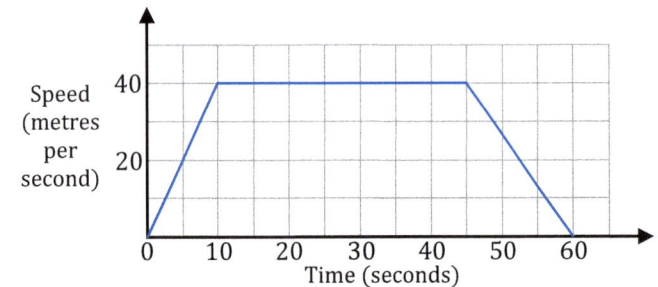

Across continued

18. Using the graph in clue 16 across, determine the speed of the car during the first 40 seconds in m/s. Subtract the speed during this time from 700 m/s
19. Using the graph in clue 13 down, determine the number of seconds for which the train was travelling at a constant speed. Subtract the time found from 295 seconds

Down continued

14. Using the graph in clue 13 down, determine the acceleration of the train during the first 10 seconds in m/s². Subtract the acceleration during this time from 114 m/s²
17. Using the graph in clue 13 down, determine the number of seconds for which the train was accelerating

Iterations and Sequences

Examples	Solutions
An iterative process is given by $x_{n+1} = \sqrt[3]{8 - 2x_n}$ and $x_0 = 1.5$. Find the solution to 2 decimal places	$x_1 = \sqrt[3]{8 - 2(1.5)} = 1.709..$, $x_2 = \sqrt[3]{8 - 2(x_1)} = 1.660..$, $x_3 = 1.672..$, $x_4 = 1.669..$ Therefore, to 2 decimal places $x = 1.67$
The first four terms in an arithmetic sequence are 2, 5, 8, 11. What is the 12th term of the sequence?	The common difference between terms is 3, which is the coefficient of n in the nth term. The nth term is $U_n = 3n - 1$. $U_{12} = 3(12) - 1 = 35$. This is a position-to-term sequence as each term is calculated based on its position in the sequence
What is the next term in the geometric sequence 4, 12, 36, 108?	To find each term multiply the previous term by 3. $U_{n+1} = 3U_n$. The 5th term is $U_5 = 3U_4 = 3(108) = 324$. This is a term-to-term sequence as each term is calculated based on the previous term in the sequence
Find the position-to-term formula U_n for the quadratic sequence 3, 11, 23, 39	Quadratic sequences take the form of $U_n = an^2 + bn + c$. Substituting in $n = 1, 2$ and 3 gives three equations: Eq 1: $a + b + c = 3$. Eq 2: $4a + 2b + c = 11$. Eq 3: $9a + 3b + c = 23$. Solving gives $U_n = 2n^2 + 2n - 1$

Real-Life Graphs

Examples	Solutions
A car journey is shown on the distance-time graph. How long was the car stationary? What was the speed of the car in the first 50 seconds?	The car was stationary where the line is horizontal, which was for $25 + 75 = 100$ seconds. Speed given by the gradient of the graph $= \frac{500 - 0}{50 - 0} = 10$ m/s
A train journey is shown on the speed-time graph. How long was the train accelerating, at a constant speed and decelerating? What was the acceleration of the train in the first 20 seconds? What was the total distance travelled by the train?	The train accelerated for the first 20 seconds, then travelled at a constant speed for 10 seconds before decelerating for 15 seconds. Acceleration = gradient of the graph $= \frac{60 - 0}{20 - 0} = 3$ m/s². Distance = area under graph $= \frac{a+b}{2} h = \frac{10 + 45}{2}(60) = 1650$ m

Crossword 13: Chapter 2 Consolidation Crossword

Across

2. Expand $5(2y + 6) - 8(5y - 11)$ fully and simplify the result into the form $ay + b$. What is the value of b?
4. Factorise $100x^2 - 4$ fully into the form $a(bx + 1)(bx - 1)$. What is the result of subtracting the value of b from 224?
6. Make x the subject of $y = \frac{x - 1021}{1 + x}$. What is the value of x when $y = -1$?
7. A parallelogram and a rectangle are shown below. The perimeters of the shapes are equal. All measurements are in centimetres. What is the total area (in cm²) of 8 such rectangles identical to that shown below?

Not to scale

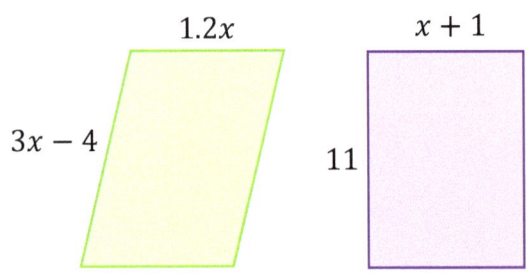

9. Find the equation of the straight line which passes through $(-3, -2)$ and $(3, 4)$. Point $P(19, k)$ lies on the line. Work out k

Down

1. Form an expression for the area of the triangle and simplify the expression into the form $ax^2 + \frac{b}{c}x + d$. Multiply the value of $\frac{b}{c}$ by 100 and write the result in the grid

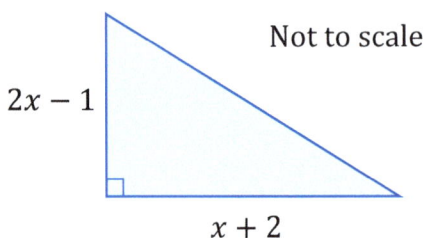

Not to scale

2. Solve $2(x - 6) = 3x - 118$
3. Solve $\frac{8}{x} + \frac{4}{x + 2} = 5$. Multiply the largest solution by 4325 and write the result in the grid
4. Smallest integer that satisfies $7x - 119 > 6x + 158$
5. Solve the simultaneous equations below. Subtract the value of x from 9340 and write the result in the grid

$$2x + 11y = 51$$
$$x - 5y = -6$$

8. Find the equation of straight line A which passes through $(200, 200)$ and is parallel to $y = -4x + 3$. At what y-coordinate does line A intersect the y-axis?

Across continued

10. Determine the midpoint coordinates of the straight line with end point coordinates $(-5, 2)$ and $(27, 8)$. Write the x-coordinate of the midpoint coordinates in the grid
11. The area of the symmetrical trapezium is six times the area of the square. All sides are measured in metres. What is the perimeter of the square in millimetres?

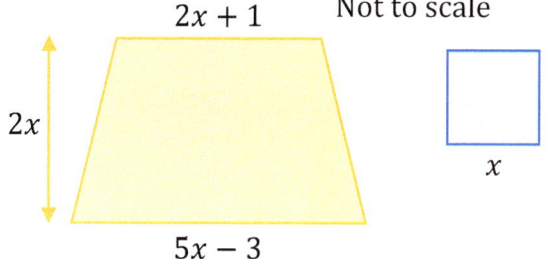

12. Solve $x^2 - 9x + 4 = 0$. Round the largest solution to the nearest whole number. Take the rounded number away from 351 and write the result in the grid
13. Solve the simultaneous equations below. Add 473 to the largest solution for x and write the result in the grid

$$y + 5x = -3$$
$$y + x^2 = 3$$

15. If $f(x) = 3 + 2x$ and $g(x) = 2x^2 - 8$, find $gf(10)$
17. The area of the rectangle is 64 cm². What is the value of k?

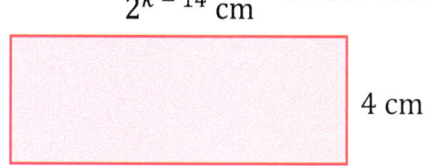

18. An iterative process is given by $x_{n+1} = \sqrt[3]{70 + 30x_n}$ and $x_0 = 7$. Calculate x_3 rounded to 1 decimal place. Multiply the rounded solution by 10
20. A train journey is shown on the graph. How many metres did the train travel in total?

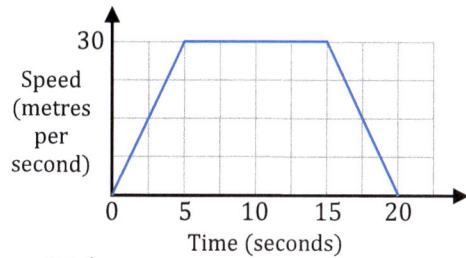

21. Solve $\frac{x+1}{60} = 10$

Down continued

9. Find the equation of straight line B which passes through $(300, 540)$ and is perpendicular to $y = \frac{x}{5} - 2$. At what y-coordinate does line B intersect the y-axis?
10. The graph of $y = -x + 12$ is shown below. Sketch the graph of $y = \frac{3}{4}x - 2$ on the same diagram. Hence, find the solution to the simultaneous equations $y = -x + 12$ and $y = \frac{3}{4}x - 2$. This solution occurs where both lines cross. Sum the x and y values of the solution and write the result in the grid

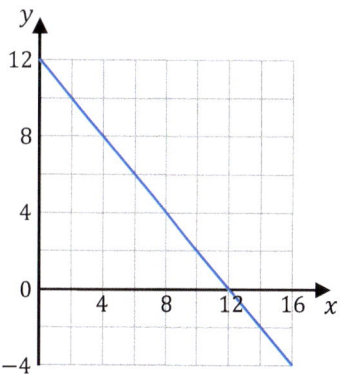

12. The function g is given by $g(x) = \frac{1}{12}x - 3$. Find the value of $g^{-1}(330)$
14. Solve $x^2 + 16x + 21 = 0$ by completing the square. Express the solution in the form $a \pm \sqrt{b}$. Add 1826 to the value of b and write the result in the grid
15. If $f(x) = -x^2 + 7x + 255$, at what value does the graph of $y = f(x) - 78$ intersect the y-axis?
16. The first four terms in an arithmetic sequence are 14, 26, 38, 50. What is the 46th term of the sequence?
19. The graph below shows the quadratic equation $x^2 - 30x + 200$. A straight line is also shown. It passes through the turning point of the quadratic (point T), the origin (point O) and point P at coordinates $(-27, k)$. What is the value of k?

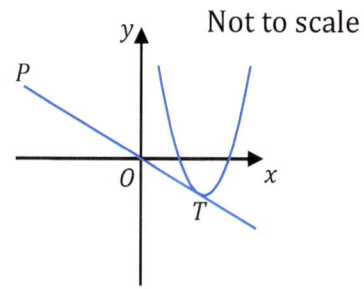

Chapter 3
Ratio, Proportion and Rates of Change

Crossword 14: Ratio, Similarity and Proportionality

Across

1. The ratio of the number of red pens to the number of green pens on a desk is 4 : 3. There are 48 red pens on the desk. How many green pens are there?
2. At a school the ratio of the number of boys to the number of girls is 5 : 7. There are 136 more girls than boys. How many students in total are at the school?
4. Given that $3x - 8 : 8x + 19 = 2 : 9$, determine the value of x
5. Cyril sells 10 litre pots of green paint for £57 each. To make the green paint he mixes yellow paint (costing £3.85 per litre) and blue paint (costing £4.10 per litre) in the ratio 2 : 3. How much profit in pounds (£) does Cyril make on each 10 litre pot of green paint?
6. Two similar cones have heights in the ratio 5 : 6. Determine the ratio $x : y$ of their volumes. Write the value of y in the grid
8. Two 3D shapes S1 and S2 are similar. The ratio of the surface area of S1 to the surface area of S2 is 4 : 25. The volume of S2 is 625 cm³. What is the volume of S1 in cm³?
9. Which graph is a sketch of $y \propto x$? Write the number under the correct graph in the grid

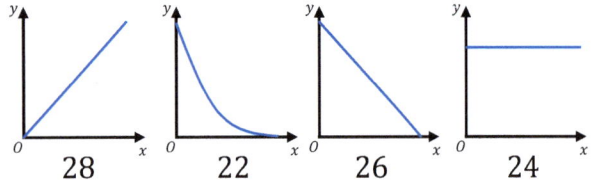

Down

1. The ratio of the number of adults to the number of children in a supermarket is 5 : 2. There are 92 children in the supermarket. How many people are in the supermarket?
2. A footballer scored 240 goals. 20% of her goals were scored through headers and the remainder were scored using either her right or left foot in the ratio 1 : 2. How many more goals did she score with her left foot than she scored with headers?
3. Jane is making biscuits. Three ingredients, butter, sugar and flour are mixed in the ratio 2 : 2 : 3 to make the cake mixture. Jane makes 2.135 kg of mixture. How many grams of sugar does she use?
4. In a bag of marbles there are four times as many yellow marbles as purple marbles and twice as many purple marbles as blue marbles. If there are 2 blue marbles in the bag, how many yellow marbles are there?
7. Work out 20% of 5.3 m² in cm²
8. The two rectangles below are similar. What is the area of the smaller rectangle in cm²?

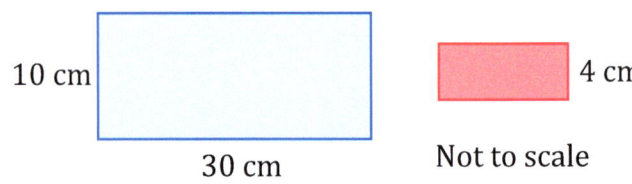

9. Two similar cylinders (C1 and C2) have volumes in the ratio 64 : 27. If the height of C1 is 34 cm, what is the height of C2 in mm?

Across continued

11. If a is directly proportional to b^3 and $a = 40$ when $b = 2$, find the value of a when $b = 9$
12. If c is inversely proportional to d^2 and $c = 5$ when $d = 4$, what is the value of c when $d = 2$?
13. If y is directly proportional to $\sqrt{x}$ and $y = 36$ when $x = 81$, what is the value of y when $x = 20449$?
14. If y is inversely proportional to x and $y = 50$ when $x = 10$. Find the value of y when $x = 5$
15. The table shows some values for which y is directly proportional to x^2. p, q and r are positive integers. Find the sum of p, q and r

x	1	p	8	4
y	0.5	2	q	r

Down continued

10. The cuboids below are similar. What is the length of the edge labelled x in mm?

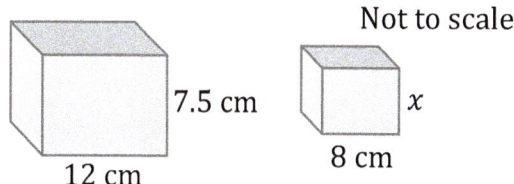

Not to scale

12. Using the cuboids in clue 10 down, if the volume of the larger cuboid is 756 cm³, what is the volume of the smaller cuboid in cm³?

Ratio and Similarity

Examples	Solutions
Lesley, Paul and Nina shared 60 apples in the ratio 2 : 3 : 5. How many apples did Paul get?	60 apples are equal to $2 + 3 + 5 = 10$ parts. 1 part = $60 \div 10 = 6$ apples. Therefore, Paul got $3 \times 6 = 18$ apples
The ratio of the number of small cards to the number of large cards is 4 : 9. There are 260 more large cards than small cards. How many cards are there in total?	The 260 large cards make up $9 - 4 = 5$ more parts of the ratio than the small cards. 1 part = $260 \div 5 = 52$ cards. Total cards = $(4 \times 52) + (9 \times 52) = 676$
Given that $2x + 5 : 4 - x = 3 : 5$, determine the value of x	$\frac{2x+5}{4-x} = \frac{3}{5} \Rightarrow 5(2x+5) = 3(4-x) \Rightarrow x = -1$
Rectangle R1 has length 40 m and width 12 m. Rectangle R2 has length 8 m and width x. R1 and R2 are similar. Find the area of R2 in m² and from this convert the area directly to cm²	$\frac{8}{40} = \frac{x}{12} \Rightarrow 40x = 96 \Rightarrow x = 2.4$ m. Area of R2 = $8 \times 2.4 = 19.2$ m². Area in cm² = $19.2 \times 100 \times 100 = 192000$ cm² as 1 m = 100 cm
Two similar spheres (S1 and S2) have volumes in the ratio 64 : 125. If the radius of S2 is 20 cm, what is the radius of S1 in cm?	Linear scale factor = $\sqrt[3]{64} : \sqrt[3]{125} = 4 : 5$. Surface area scale factor = $4^2 : 5^2 = 16 : 25$. Radius of S1 = $\frac{4}{5} \times 20 = 16$ cm

Proportionality

If y and x are directly proportional, $y \propto x \Rightarrow y = kx$. Therefore, as x increases, y increases.
If y and x are inversely proportional, $y \propto \frac{1}{x} \Rightarrow y = \frac{k}{x}$. Therefore, as x increases, y decreases

Examples	Solutions
If y is directly proportional to x^2 and $y = 150$ when $x = 5$, find the value of y when $x = 7$	$y = kx^2 \Rightarrow k = y \div x^2 = 150 \div 5^2 = 6$. Therefore, $y = 6x^2 = 6(7^2) = 294$
If a is inversely proportional to $\sqrt{b}$ and $a = 2$ when $b = 16$, find the value of a when $b = 36$	$a = \frac{k}{\sqrt{b}} \Rightarrow k = a\sqrt{b} = 2(\sqrt{16}) = 8$. Therefore, $a = \frac{8}{\sqrt{b}} = \frac{8}{\sqrt{36}} = \frac{8}{6} = \frac{4}{3}$

Crossword 15: Rates of Change and Compound Measures

Across

1. The speed-time graph for an animal running is given by the blue line. The red line represents a tangent to the curve at $t = 4$. Work out the gradient of the red line to 1 decimal place. Multiply the rounded answer by 20 and write the result in the grid

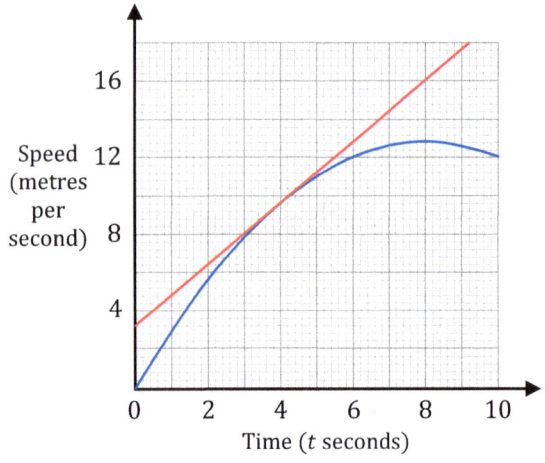

3. Using the graph in clue 1 across, work out an estimate for the distance travelled by the animal in the first 10 seconds. Use 5 strips of equal width and give your answer in metres
5. Using the graph in clue 1 across, work out the average acceleration in m/s² during the 10 seconds. Multiply the answer by 100 and write the result in the grid
6. What is 27.5 m/s in km/h?
7. Carole drove for 80 minutes at an average speed of 45 km/h. How far did Carole drive in km?
8. Calculate the force acting on an object in newtons (N) if a pressure of 121750 N/m² is applied to an area of 40 cm²

Down

2. The distance-time graph for a slow-moving vehicle is given by the purple line. Work out the vehicle's average speed in m/s during the 10 seconds. Multiply the answer by 21 and write the result in the grid

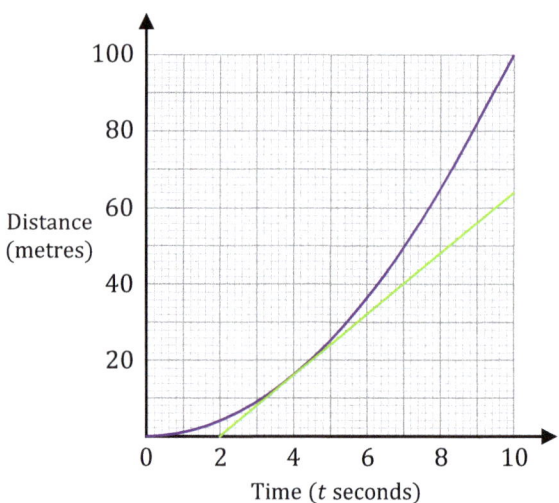

3. The green line on the graph above represents a tangent to the curve at $t = 4$. Work out the gradient of the green line. Multiply the gradient value by 1130 and write the result in the grid
4. What is 70 km/h in m/s? Give your answer correct to the nearest whole number
6. Harry walks at an average speed of 5.6 miles per hour. How many seconds will it take Harry to walk 1.512 miles?
9. A force of 60 newtons (N) acts on a circle of radius 12 cm. Calculate the pressure produced by this force on the circle in N/m². Give your answer to the nearest whole number

Across continued

9. 120 g of metal A is mixed with 160 g of metal B to make an alloy. The density of metal A is 8 g/cm³ and the density of metal B is 13 g/cm³. To the nearest whole number, what is the density of the alloy in g/cm³?
10. A set of headphones worth £51 depreciates by 20% each year for four years. What is its value to the nearest pound at the end of the four years?
12. Using the information in clue 12 down, determine to the nearest whole number of pounds, the profit that Anna would make by investing in account C for three years
14. The population of a city is increasing at a constant rate of 3.6% each year. At the end of 2017 the population was 24951. What will be the population to the nearest whole number of people by the end of 2021?

Down continued

11. A cube of metal with edge length 0.75 m has a density of 3.4 g/cm³. What is the mass of the cube? Give your answer to the nearest kg
12. Anna has £5000 which she wishes to invest for three years. She has three account options to choose from. Account A pays simple interest at 2% per year, account B pays compound interest at 1.8% per year and account C pays 3% interest in year 1, 2% interest in year 2 and 1.9% interest in year 3. How many pounds profit would Anna make by investing in account A for three years?
13. Using the information in clue 12 down, determine to the nearest whole number of pounds, the profit that Anna would make by investing in account B for three years

Rates of Change

The blue line on the graph represents a speed-time curve.

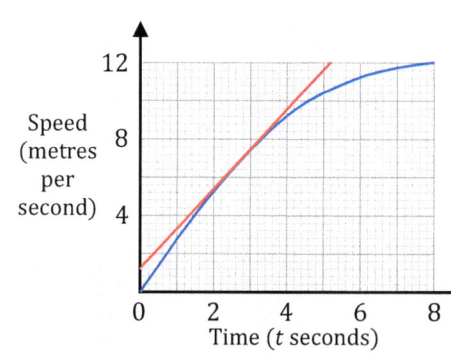

Acceleration (A) at $t = 3$ seconds is given by the gradient of the red tangent line. $A = \frac{12 - 1.2}{5.2 - 0} = 2.1$ m/s² to 1 decimal place.

Average acceleration over 8 seconds is given by the gradient between the two end points of the curve $= \frac{12 - 0}{8 - 0} = 1.5$ m/s².

Distance (D) travelled in 8 seconds is given by the area under the curve, which can be approximated using 4 trapeziums.
$D = \frac{1}{2}(0 + 5.2)(2) + \frac{1}{2}(5.2 + 9.2)(2) + \frac{1}{2}(9.2 + 11.2)(2) + \frac{1}{2}(11.2 + 12)(2) = 63.2$ m

Note: for a distance-time graph the gradient gives speed instead of acceleration

Compound Measures

Examples	Solutions
What is 115 km/h in m/s?	115 km in 1 hour = 115000 m in 3600 seconds = $\frac{115000}{3600}$ = 31.9 metres per second to 1 decimal place
Tom drove for 95 minutes at an average speed of 50 km/h. How far did Tom drive?	Speed = $\frac{\text{distance}}{\text{time}}$ ⇒ distance = speed × time = $50 \times \frac{95}{60}$ = 79.2 km to 1 decimal place
A force of 100 newtons (N) acts on an area of 250 cm². What pressure in N/m² is applied on the area?	Pressure = $\frac{\text{force}}{\text{area}}$ = $\frac{100}{0.025}$ = 4000 N/m²
160 g of metal A with density 10 g/cm³ is mixed with 186 g of metal B with density 12 g/cm³ to make an alloy. What is the density of the alloy in g/cm³?	Volume of A = $\frac{\text{mass}}{\text{density}}$ = $\frac{160}{10}$ = 16, and B = $\frac{186}{12}$ = 15.5. Density of alloy = $\frac{\text{mass}}{\text{volume}}$ = $\frac{(160 + 186)}{(16 + 15.5)}$ ≈ 11 g/cm³
Work out the simple and compound interest of investing £150 for 4 years in accounts offering 5% each year	Simple interest = $4 \times ((1.05 \times £150) - £150)$ = £30. Compound interest = $((1.05)^4 \times £150) - £150$ = £32 to the nearest pound

Crossword 16: Chapter 3 Consolidation Crossword

Across

1. The ratio of the number of fiction books to the number of non-fiction books in a warehouse is 9 : 16. There are 675 fiction books. How many books (fiction and non-fiction) are there in total?
3. Roy produces and sells 2 litre bottles of fizzy orange drink for £3.90 each. The drink is made up of orange cordial (costing £1.25 per 500 millilitres) and sparkling water (costing 40 pence per 500 millilitres) in the ratio 1 : 3. Ignoring the cost of the bottles, how much profit in pence (p) does Roy make on each bottle of fizzy orange drink?
5. Given that $3x + 2 : x + 5 = x - 2 : 2x - 13$, determine the possible values of x. Multiply the largest value of x by 3.625 and write the result in the grid
7. The two right-angled triangles below are mathematically similar. What is the area of the larger triangle in cm²?

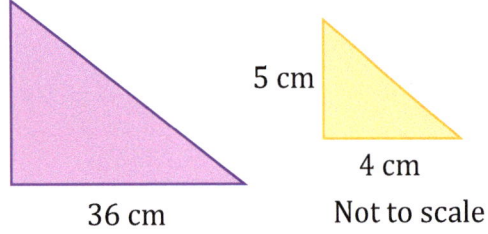

36 cm, 5 cm, 4 cm, Not to scale

Down

1. An amount of money was shared between Karl, Janya and Isaac in the ratio 3 : 2 : 7. Isaac received £160 more than Janya. How many more pounds did Isaac receive compared to Karl?
2. The ratio of the number of 2D shapes to the number of 3D shapes drawn on a piece of paper is 4 : 3. 70% of the 2D shapes are coloured yellow and 28% of the 3D shapes are coloured yellow. What percentage of all the shapes on the paper are coloured yellow?
3. Sugar, syrup and butter are mixed in the ratio 8 : 7 : 5 to make a sweet mixture. A 200 g bag of sugar costs 50 pence, a 250 g pot of syrup costs 80 pence and a 250 g pot of butter costs £1.60. Jennifer uses up 5 kg of mixture to make sweets. Each sweet weighs 10 g and sells for 4 pence. How much profit in pence (p) will Jennifer make by selling all the sweets?
4. The ratio of the time it takes to complete task A to the time it takes to complete task B is given by $x : 3$. When x is increased by 22, the ratio becomes 8 : 1. Find the value of x and use it to determine the number of minutes it will take to complete task B if task A is completed in 3500 minutes

Across continued

9. Two similar pentagonal prisms (P1 and P2) are shown below. The surface areas are: P1 = 461 cm² and P2 = 165 cm². If the volume of P2 is 135 cm³, what is the volume of P1 in cm³ to the nearest whole number?

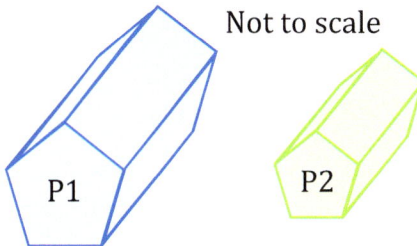

Not to scale

10. Two similar cubes (C1 and C2) have volumes in the ratio 125 : 729. If the width of C2 is 54 cm, what is the width of C1 in cm?
11. If y is directly proportional to x and $y = 6$ when $x = 3$, find the value of y when $x = 35$
12. If y is inversely proportional to x and $y = 23$ when $x = 9$. Find the value of y when $x = \frac{1}{6}$
14. The population of a town is decreasing at a constant rate of 0.6% each year. At the end of 2016 the population was 4000. To the nearest whole number of people, how many fewer people will be in the town by the end of 2022?
15. Using the graph in clue 11 down, work out an estimate for the distance travelled in metres during the first 6 seconds. Use 6 strips of equal width and round your answer to the nearest metre
17. y is inversely proportional to x. If x decreases by 43%, to the nearest whole number, what percentage will y increase by?
18. 170 g of metal A is mixed with 220 g of metal B to make an alloy. The density of metal A is 48 g/cm³ and the density of metal B is 76 g/cm³. To the nearest whole number, what is the density of the alloy in g/cm³?
20. Work out the total compound interest made in pounds (£) of investing £1548 for 4 years offering 12% interest each year. Give your answer to the nearest pound
21. A force of 18.1 newtons acts on an area of 500 cm². What pressure in N/m² is applied?
23. Akari invested £100 in an account paying compound interest at the rate of x% each year. At the end of the second year the account totals £143.35. To the nearest pound, how many pounds will be in the account at the end of 3 years?

Down continued

6. Two similar parallelograms are shown below. If $a = 8$ cm, $b = 15$ cm and $c = 24$ cm, what is the area of the shaded region in cm²?

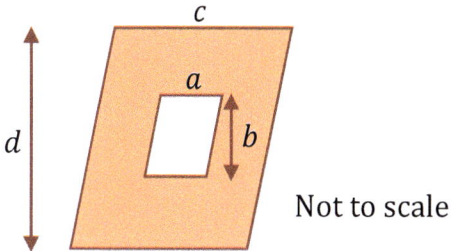

Not to scale

8. Work out 32% of 6 cm² in mm²
10. Which graph is a sketch of $y \propto \frac{1}{x}$? Write the number under the correct graph in the grid

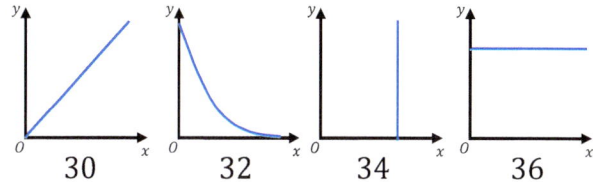

11. Work out the gradient of the red line below to the nearest whole number. Multiply the rounded value by 1824 and write the result in the grid

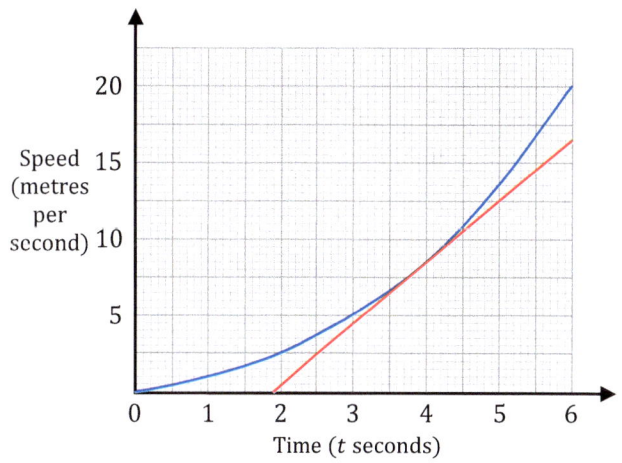

13. Using the blue line on the graph in clue 11 down, work out the average acceleration in m/s² during the 6 seconds to the nearest whole number. Add the rounded answer to 49778 m/s² and write the result in the grid
14. What is 310 m/s in km/h?
16. A force of 66 newtons (N) acts on an area of 750 cm². What pressure in N/m² is applied?
19. A metal of mass 1000 g has a density of 8 g/cm³. What is its volume in cm³?
21. Kathy drove 96 miles in 180 minutes. What was her average speed in miles per hour?
22. Work out the total simple interest made in pounds (£) of investing £320 for 3 years offering 2.5% interest each year

Chapter 4
Geometry and Measures

Crossword 17: Angles, Congruency, Area and Perimeter

Across

1. What is the size of angle x?

   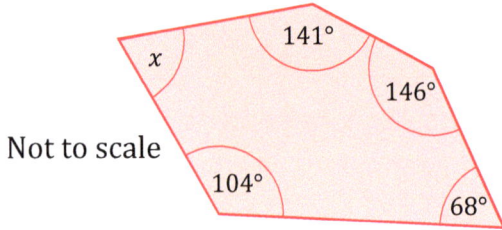

   Not to scale

3. A regular heptagon and a regular decagon are shown in the diagram below. Find the size of angle x to the nearest whole number. Multiply the rounded value of x by 7 and write the result in the grid

   Not to scale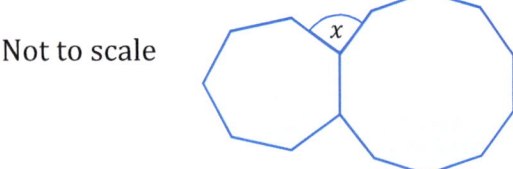

6. Lines ABC, DEFG and HIJ are parallel. BF = IF and BE = IE. Given that $u = 15°$. What is the size of reflex angle x?

   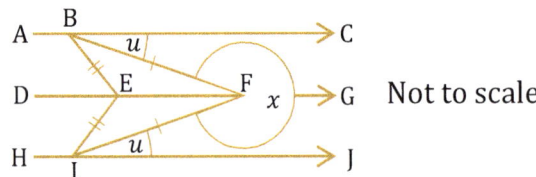 Not to scale

7. Triangles T5 and T6 are congruent because of SAS. What is the size of angle b?

   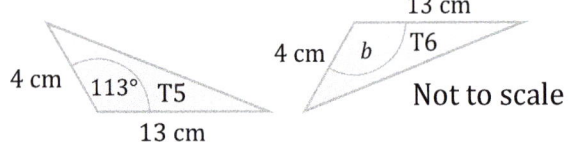 Not to scale

Down

2. Three straight lines AB, CD and EF are shown below. Lines AB and CD are parallel. All angles on the diagram are in degrees. What is the size of angle y?

   Not to scale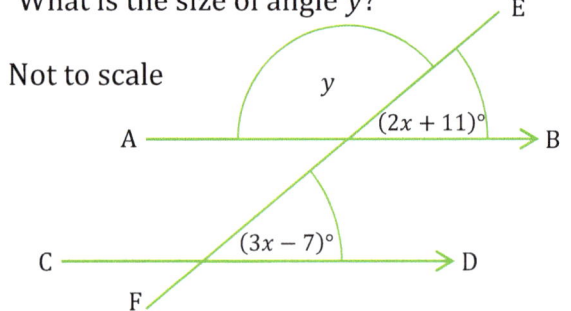

3. What is the exterior angle size of a regular hexagon? (Exterior angle = $360° \div n$, where n is the number of sides on the polygon)

4. Lines ABC and DEFG are parallel. BE = BF. Find the size of angle x. Multiply the value of x by 14 and write the result in the grid

   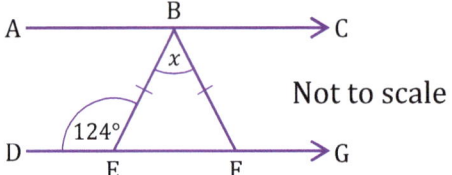

   Not to scale

5. Triangles T1 and T2 are congruent because of SSS. What is the perimeter of T2 in cm?

   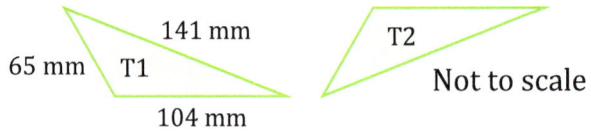 Not to scale

8. Triangles T3 and T4 are congruent because of RHS. What is the hypotenuse of T3 in mm?

   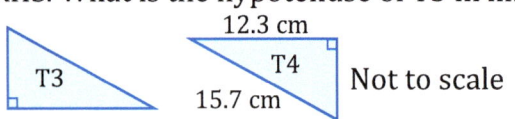 Not to scale

Across continued

9. The perimeters of the rectangle and regular hexagon below are equal. All measurements are in centimetres. Form a simplified expression for the side length of the hexagon in terms of x and find its side length in millimetres if $x = 6$

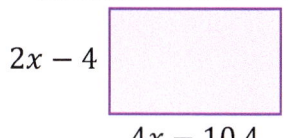
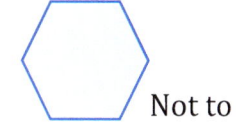
Not to scale

10. What is the perimeter of the hexagon in clue 9 across? Give your answer in millimetres
11. A right-angled triangle has base 55 cm and perpendicular height 1 cm. What is its area in mm²?
14. Find the area of the rectangle in clue 9 across in cm² (assume again that $x = 6$). Give your answer to 2 significant figures
15. The area of a parallelogram is given by $A = bh$. If $A = 7$ m² and $b = 125$ cm, what is h in centimetres?

Down continued

9. A rectangle and symmetrical trapezium are below. All measurements are in centimetres. The area of the rectangle is 40 cm². What is the area of the trapezium in cm²?

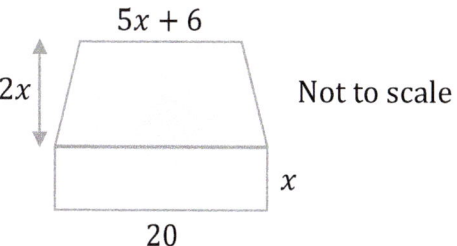
Not to scale

10. What is the perimeter of a square with side length 0.1 metres? Give your answer in cm
11. To the nearest whole number, what is the combined area in cm² of 10 triangles identical to triangle T5 in clue 7 across?
12. Given that BE = 33 cm, to the nearest whole number, what is the area in cm² of triangle BEF in clue 4 down?
13. To the nearest whole number, what is the area in cm² of triangle T4 in clue 8 down?
14. How many sides does a decagon have?

Angles and Congruency

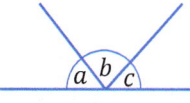
Angles on a straight line sum to 180°.
$a + b + c = 180°$

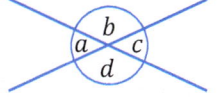
Angles at a point sum to 360°.
$a + b + c + d = 360°$

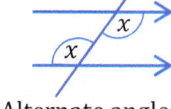
Alternate angles (x) are equal

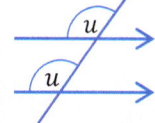
Corresponding angles (u) are equal

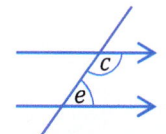
Supplementary angles sum to 180°. i.e. $c + e = 180°$

Polygon name	Triangle	Quadrilateral	Pentagon	Hexagon	Heptagon	Octagon	Nonagon	Decagon
Number of sides	3	4	5	6	7	8	9	10
Sum of interior angles	180°	360°	540°	720°	900°	1080°	1260°	1440°

Congruent triangles are identical to each other. Two triangles are congruent if at least 1 of these 4 conditions is true:

SSS: 3 sides are equal

SAS: 2 sides and included angle are equal

RHS: Right angled, hypotenuse and 1 other side are equal

ASA: 2 angles and corresponding side equal

Area and Perimeter

The formulas for the area (A) and perimeter (P) of some common shapes are shown below

Triangle (right-angled)	Triangle (any type)	Square	Rectangle	Parallelogram	Symmetrical trapezium
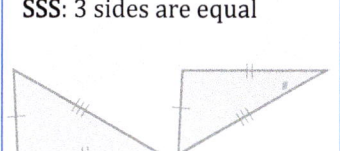	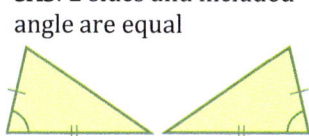		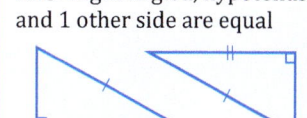		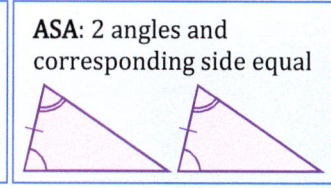
$A = \frac{1}{2}bh$	$A = \frac{1}{2}ab \sin C$	$A = a^2$	$A = ah$	$A = ah$	$A = \frac{1}{2}(a+b)h$
$P = b + c + h$	$P = a + b + c$	$P = 4a$	$P = 2a + 2h$	$P = 2a + 2b$	$P = a + b + 2c$

Crossword 18: Vectors and Transformations

Note: assume that values m, n and k are always integers in this crossword

Across

1. If $\mathbf{a} = \begin{pmatrix} 5 \\ 4 \end{pmatrix}$ and $\mathbf{b} = \begin{pmatrix} 7 \\ 10 \end{pmatrix}$, determine the vector $\mathbf{a} + \mathbf{b}$ in the format $\begin{pmatrix} m \\ n \end{pmatrix}$. Write the product of values m and n in the grid

3. Vectors $\mathbf{a}$, $\mathbf{b}$, $\mathbf{c}$ and $\mathbf{d}$ are drawn on the diagram below. Find vector $\mathbf{c}$ in terms of $\mathbf{a}$ in the form $k\mathbf{a}$. Multiply the value of k by 9 and write the result in the grid

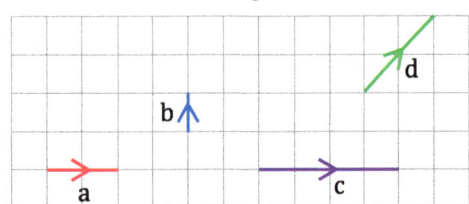

5. OAB is a triangle. C is the point on AB such that $AC : CB = 2 : 5$. $\overrightarrow{OA} = 21\mathbf{a}$ and $\overrightarrow{OB} = 14\mathbf{b}$. Find $\overrightarrow{OC}$ in the form $k\mathbf{a} + n\mathbf{b}$. Then find the value of $4(k - n)$ and write the result in the grid

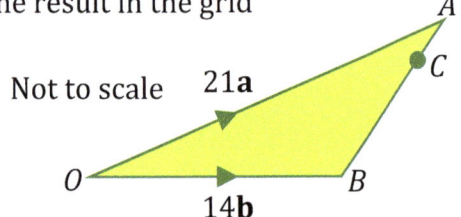

Not to scale

6. $OABC$ is a rectangle. D is the point on BC such that $BD : DC = 4 : 1$. $\overrightarrow{AO} = 10\mathbf{a}$ and $\overrightarrow{OC} = 25\mathbf{b}$. Find $\overrightarrow{AD}$ in the form $k\mathbf{a} + n\mathbf{b}$. Multiply the value of n by 469 and write the result in the grid

Not to scale

Down

2. If $\mathbf{a} = \begin{pmatrix} 2 \\ -9 \end{pmatrix}$ and $\mathbf{b} = \begin{pmatrix} -3 \\ -7 \end{pmatrix}$, find the vector $\mathbf{a} - \mathbf{b}$ in the format $\begin{pmatrix} m \\ n \end{pmatrix}$. Add the value of n to 639 and write the result in the grid

3. Using the diagram in clue 3 across, find vector $\mathbf{d}$ in terms of $\mathbf{a}$ and $\mathbf{b}$ in the form $k\mathbf{a} + n\mathbf{b}$. Subtract the value of n from 16 and write the result in the grid

4. OAB is a triangle. C is the midpoint of AB. $\overrightarrow{OA} = 6\mathbf{a}$ and $\overrightarrow{OB} = 4\mathbf{b}$. Find $\overrightarrow{OC}$ in the form $k\mathbf{a} + n\mathbf{b}$. Multiply the value of k by 7 and write the result in the grid

Not to scale

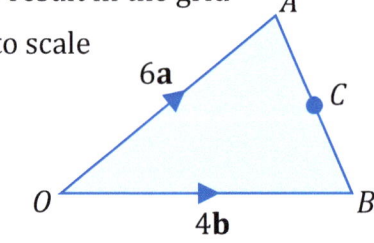

5. Using the diagram in clue 6 across, find $\overrightarrow{CA}$ in the form $k\mathbf{a} + n\mathbf{b}$. Then find the value of $3(k - n)$ and write the result in the grid

7. $OABC$ is a symmetrical trapezium. $\overrightarrow{AB} = 8\mathbf{a}$, $\overrightarrow{AO} = 5\mathbf{b}$ and $\overrightarrow{OC} = 11\mathbf{a}$. Find $\overrightarrow{BC}$ in the form $k\mathbf{a} + n\mathbf{b}$. Multiply the value of n by 20 and write the result in the grid

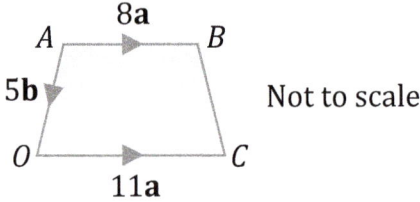

Not to scale

8. How many times longer is $\overrightarrow{YZ}$ than $\overrightarrow{WX}$ if $\overrightarrow{WX} = 3\mathbf{a}$ and $\overrightarrow{YZ} = 756\mathbf{a}$?

Across continued

10. Translate shape A by the vector $\begin{pmatrix} -5 \\ 1 \end{pmatrix}$ and label it as shape B on the diagram below. Multiply the y-coordinate for the centre of shape B by 6 and write the result in the grid

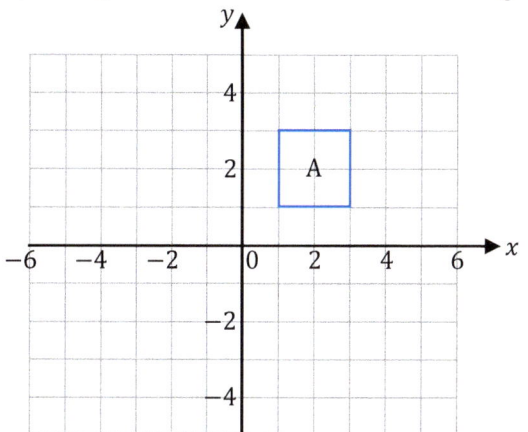

11. On the diagram above, reflect shape A in the line $y = -1$ and label it shape C. Multiply the y-coordinate for the centre of shape C by -10 and write the result in the grid
12. On the diagram above, rotate shape A 180° about $(3, 3)$ and label it shape D. Multiply the x-coordinate for the centre of shape D by 7 and write the result in the grid
15. Following the rotation in clue 12 across, subtract the number of invariant corners on shape D from 647
17. On the diagram above, enlarge shape A by a scale factor of -2, centre $(0, 1)$ and label it shape E. Multiply the x-coordinate for the centre of shape E by -300 and write the result in the grid

Down continued

9. Translate shape V by the vector $\begin{pmatrix} 3 \\ -1 \end{pmatrix}$ and label it as shape W on the diagram below. Multiply the x-coordinate for the bottom left corner of shape W by 724 and write the result in the grid

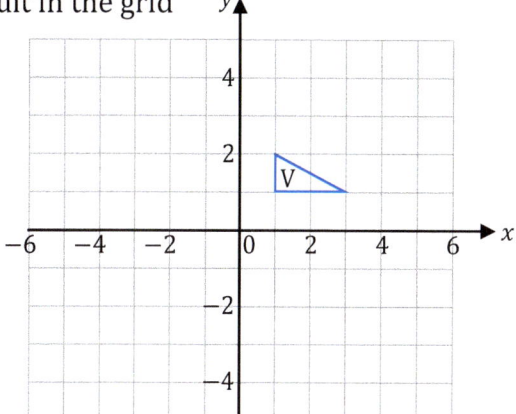

11. On the diagram above, reflect shape V in the line $x = 1$ and label it shape X. Add the y-coordinate for the top right corner of shape X to 479 and write the total in the grid
13. Following the reflection in clue 11 down, subtract the number of invariant corners on shape X from 88
14. On the diagram above, rotate shape V 90° anticlockwise about $(0, 0)$ and label it shape Y. Multiply the largest y-coordinate on the perimeter of Y by 30
16. On the diagram above, enlarge shape V by a scale factor of 2, centre $(0, 0)$ and label it shape Z. Multiply the x-coordinate for the bottom right corner of shape Z by 7 and write the result in the grid

Vectors

OAB is a triangle. C is the midpoint of AB and D is the point on OB such that $OD : DB = 5 : 1$. $\overrightarrow{OA} = 8\mathbf{a}$ and $\overrightarrow{OB} = 6\mathbf{b}$. Find $\overrightarrow{AB}, \overrightarrow{OC}$ and $\overrightarrow{AD}$.

$\overrightarrow{AB} = \overrightarrow{AO} + \overrightarrow{OB} = -8\mathbf{a} + 6\mathbf{b}$.
$\overrightarrow{OC} = \overrightarrow{OA} + \overrightarrow{AC} = \overrightarrow{OA} + \frac{1}{2}\overrightarrow{AB} = 8\mathbf{a} + \frac{1}{2}(-8\mathbf{a} + 6\mathbf{b}) = 4\mathbf{a} + 3\mathbf{b}$.
$\overrightarrow{AD} = \overrightarrow{AO} + \overrightarrow{OD} = \overrightarrow{AO} + \frac{5}{6}\overrightarrow{OB} = -8\mathbf{a} + \frac{5}{6}(6\mathbf{b}) = -8\mathbf{a} + 5\mathbf{b}$

Transformations

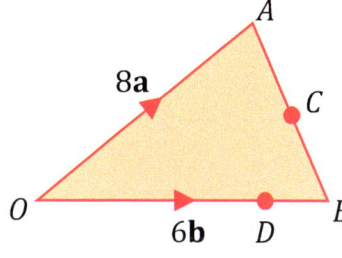

Shape A has been translated by the vector $\begin{pmatrix} -5 \\ 2 \end{pmatrix}$ to give shape B.

Shape A has been reflected in the line $y = -1$ to give shape C.

Shape A has been rotated 180° about $(-1, 1)$ to give shape D.

Shape E has been enlarged by a scale factor of -2, centre $(0, 0)$ to give shape F. Invariant points are points that remain in the same position after the transformation has taken place. For shape F, the only invariant corner is at point $(0, 0)$

Crossword 19: Circles

Across

2. To the nearest whole number, what is the circumference of the circle below in centimetres?

   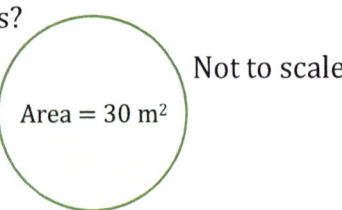
   Area = 30 m² Not to scale

4. A semicircle is shown inside a parallelogram ABCD below. The centre of the semicircle is on DC and the circumference passes through points C and D. To the nearest whole number, what is the area of the shaded region in cm²?

   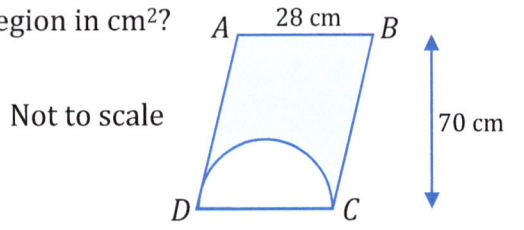
   A — 28 cm — B, 70 cm, Not to scale

6. The diagram shows a sector of a circle which has a radius of 43.05 centimetres. To the nearest whole number, what is the area of the shaded segment in cm²?

   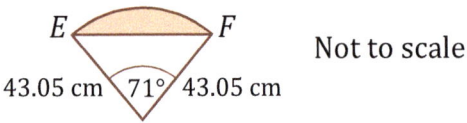
   43.05 cm 71° 43.05 cm Not to scale

8. The area of the shaded segment below is 23.64 m². To the nearest whole number, what is the radius (r) in millimetres?

   Not to scale

   r 85° r

Down

1. The diameter of a circle is 20 centimetres. To the nearest whole number, what is the area of the circle in cm²?

2. The diagram shows a sector of a circle which has a radius of 9 cm. To the nearest whole number, what is the length of arc PQ in centimetres?

   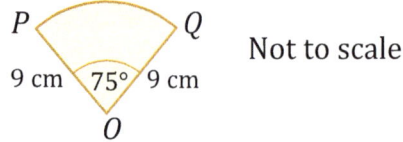
   P   Q   Not to scale
   9 cm 75° 9 cm
   O

3. Subtract the area of sector OPQ in clue 2 down from 500 cm². Give your answer in cm² to the nearest whole number

5. The diagram shows a sector of a circle which has a radius of 11 cm and $\theta = 280°$. To the nearest whole number, what is the length of arc MN in millimetres?

   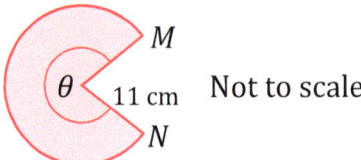
   M, θ, 11 cm, N   Not to scale

6. Subtract the area of the sector in clue 5 down from 316 cm². Give your answer in cm² to the nearest whole number

7. Two identical circles are shown inside a rectangle. To the nearest whole number, what percentage of the rectangle is shaded?

   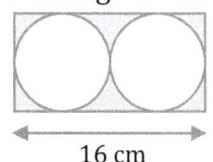
   Not to scale
   16 cm

Across continued

10. A circle with centre O is shown below. What is the size of angle w?

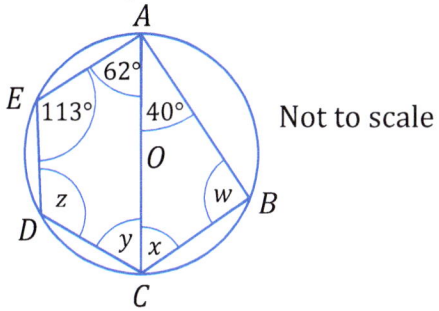

Not to scale

12. Find the size of angle x in the diagram above. Multiply the value of angle x by 27.54 and write the result in the grid
15. What is the size of angle z in the diagram above?

Down continued

8. Find the size of angle y in the diagram in clue 10 across. Subtract the value of angle y from 9098° and write the result in the grid
9. A circle with centre O is shown below. Line CTE is a tangent to the circle. Angle $CTA = 77°$ and angle $ETB = 33°$. Find the size of angle a. Add the value of angle a to 548° and write the result in the grid

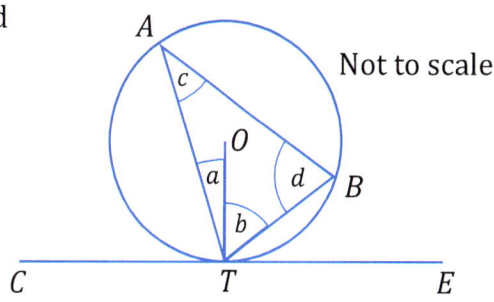

Not to scale

11. Find the size of angle b in the diagram above
13. Find the size of angle c in the diagram above
14. Find the size of angle d in the diagram above

Area, Circumference, Arcs, Sectors and Segments

Parts of a circle	Circumference/Area	Length of an arc	Area of a sector	Area of a segment
Circumference, Chord, Diameter, Radius, Centre point O, Radius = r, Diameter $d = 2r$	The circumference (C) and area (A) of a circle are given by: $C = 2\pi r$ or $C = \pi d$ $A = \pi r^2$ **Example:** If radius $r = 4$ cm $C = 2\pi(4) \approx 25$ cm $A = \pi(4)^2 \approx 50$ cm²	Arc, r, θ, r **Example:** Find the arc length when $r = 7$ m, $\theta = 62°$. $a = \frac{62°}{360°} \times 2\pi(7) \approx 8$ m	A **sector** is shown to the left. Arc length $(a) = \frac{\theta}{360°} \times 2\pi r$ Area of sector $(A) = \frac{\theta}{360°} \times \pi r^2$ **Example:** Find the area of the sector when $r = 3$ m, $\theta = 39°$. $A = \frac{39°}{360°} \times \pi(3)^2 \approx 3$ m²	Area of shaded segment = $\frac{\theta}{360°} \times \pi r^2 - \frac{1}{2} r^2 \sin\theta$

Circle Theorems

The angle in a semicircle is always equal to 90°

The perpendicular bisector of a chord passes through the circle's centre

Opposite angles of a cyclic quadrilateral sum to 180°. $a + b = 180°$ and $c + d = 180°$

The angle at the centre is twice the angle at the circumference. i.e. $y = 2x$

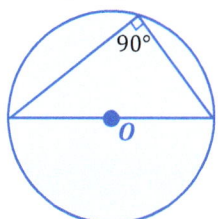  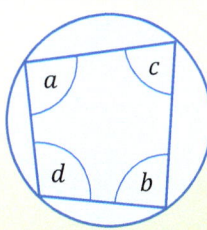 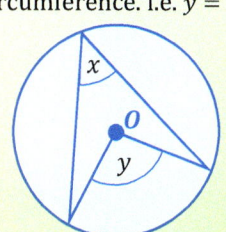

Angles in the same segment are equal. i.e. $p = q$

The angle between a radius r and a tangent T is always 90°

The lengths of tangents T and U from a point P are equal. i.e. $PT = PU$

Alternate segment theorem. $e = f$

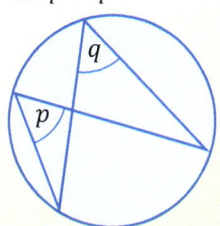 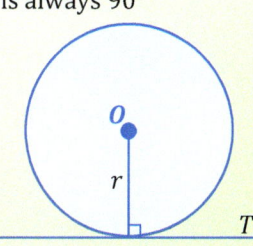 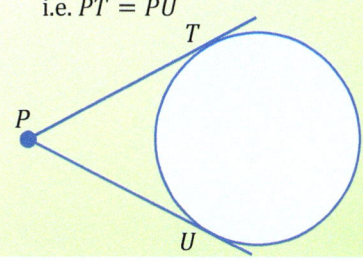 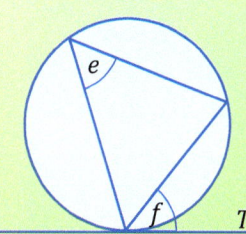

Crossword 20: Trigonometry

Across

1. To the nearest whole number, calculate the length in centimetres of side x on the right-angled triangle below

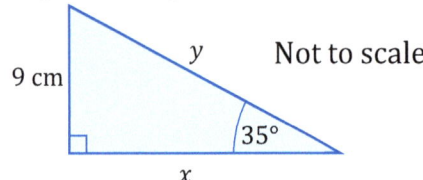

2. To the nearest whole number, calculate the length in millimetres of side y on the triangle in clue 1 across
4. Two identical right-angled triangles are shown below. To the nearest whole number, what is the perimeter of one of the triangles in centimetres?

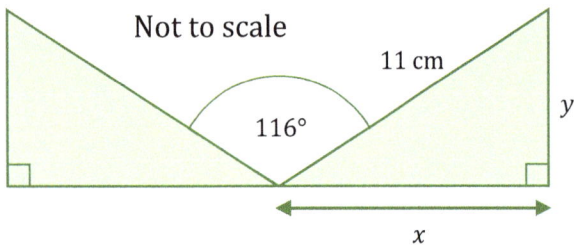

5. To the nearest whole number, what is the area of one of the triangles in clue 4 across in cm²?
6. Evaluate $1 + 72\sqrt{3} \tan 60°$
8. To the nearest whole number, what is the size of angle w below?

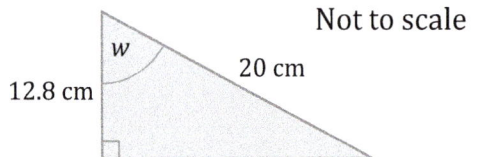

Down

1. A rectangle and a right-angled triangle are shown below. The area of the rectangle is 84 cm². To the nearest whole number, what is the base length b of the triangle in millimetres?

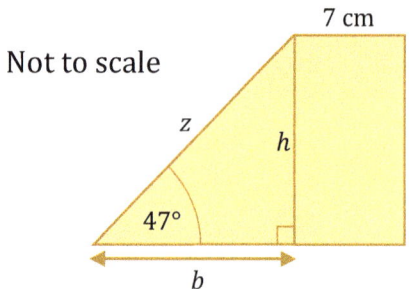

2. To the nearest whole number, calculate the length in centimetres of side z on the triangle in clue 1 down
3. Express $30 \sin 45° + 10 \cos 45°$ in the form $n\sqrt{2}$ where n is an integer. Multiply the value of n by 36 and write the result in the grid
4. Express $18 \tan 30° - 6 \sin 60°$ in the form $\sqrt{a}$ where a is an integer. Write the value of a in the grid
7. Find the area of the right-angled triangle below in the form $m\sqrt{3}$ cm², where m is an integer. Write the value of m in the grid

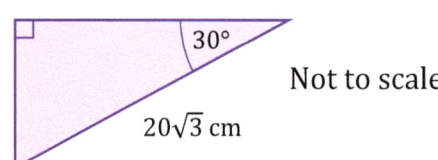

Across continued

9. To the nearest whole number, calculate the length in centimetres of side x on the triangle below

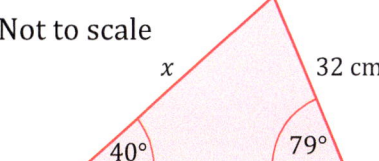
Not to scale

11. Calculate the size of angle B on the triangle in clue 8 down. Subtract the size of angle B from 243°, round the answer to the nearest whole number and write the rounded result in the grid
13. Triangles T1, T2 and T3 are shown below. To the nearest whole number, what is the length of side a on T1 in millimetres?

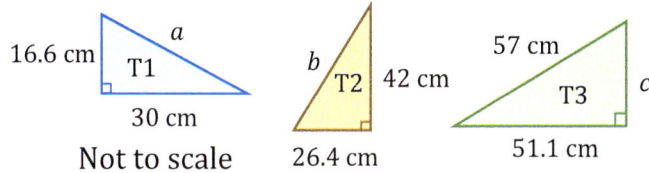
Not to scale

14. To the nearest whole number, what is the length of side b on T2 above in millimetres?
15. To the nearest whole number, what is the length of side c on T3 above in millimetres?

Down continued

8. To the nearest whole number, calculate the length in millimetres of side a on the triangle below

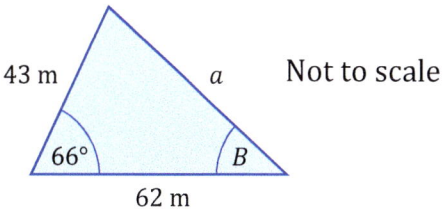
Not to scale

10. To the nearest whole number, calculate the length in centimetres of side y on triangle T5 below

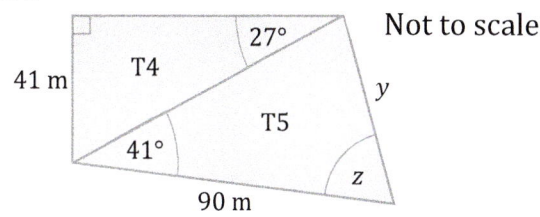
Not to scale

11. To the nearest whole number, what is the perimeter of triangle T4 above in metres?
12. To the nearest whole number, what is the perimeter of triangle T5 above in metres?

Trigonometry in Right-Angled Triangles

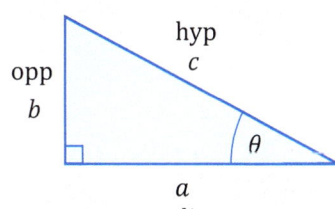

Pythagoras' Theorem: $c^2 = a^2 + b^2$

$$\sin \theta = \frac{\text{opp}}{\text{hyp}} = \frac{b}{c} \qquad \cos \theta = \frac{\text{adj}}{\text{hyp}} = \frac{a}{c} \qquad \tan \theta = \frac{\text{opp}}{\text{adj}} = \frac{b}{a}$$

Where hyp = hypotenuse, opp = opposite and adj = adjacent

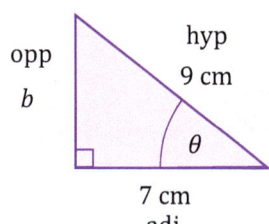

$b^2 = c^2 - a^2 = 9^2 - 7^2 = 32.$
$b = \sqrt{32} \approx 5.7$ cm.

$\cos \theta = \frac{\text{adj}}{\text{hyp}} = \frac{7}{9}, \theta = \cos^{-1}\left(\frac{7}{9}\right).$
$\theta \approx 39°$

	0°	30°	45°	60°	90°
$\sin \theta$	0	$\frac{1}{2}$	$\frac{\sqrt{2}}{2}$	$\frac{\sqrt{3}}{2}$	1
$\cos \theta$	1	$\frac{\sqrt{3}}{2}$	$\frac{\sqrt{2}}{2}$	$\frac{1}{2}$	0
$\tan \theta$	0	$\frac{\sqrt{3}}{3}$	1	$\sqrt{3}$	-

Sine and Cosine Rules

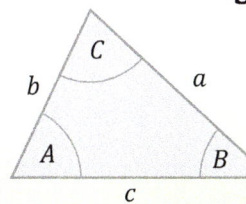

Sine rule: $\frac{a}{\sin A} = \frac{b}{\sin B} = \frac{c}{\sin C}$

Cosine rule: $a^2 = b^2 + c^2 - (2bc \cos A)$

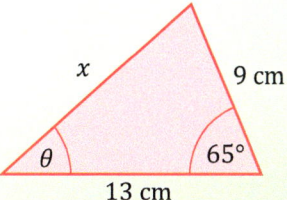

Use the Cosine Rule to find x: $x^2 = 9^2 + 13^2 - (2)(9)(13) \cos 65° = 151.10..$
Therefore, $x = \sqrt{151.10..} = 12.29..$ cm ≈ 12.3 cm.

Use the Sine Rule to find θ: $\frac{12.29..}{\sin 65°} = \frac{9}{\sin \theta} \Rightarrow \theta = \sin^{-1}\left(\frac{9}{12.29..} \times \sin 65°\right) \approx 42°$

Crossword 21: 3D Shapes, Surface Area and Volume

Across

2. What is the volume of the cuboid in cm³?

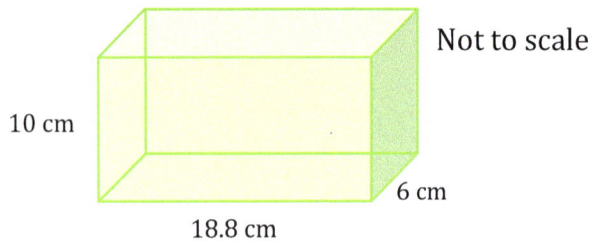
Not to scale

5. To the nearest whole number, what is the surface area of the cuboid above in cm²?
7. A triangular prism is shown below. The triangular face at each end of the prism is an equilateral triangle of side length 6 cm. To the nearest whole number, what is the volume of the prism in cm³?

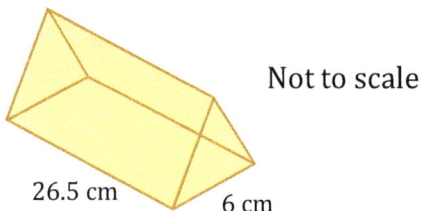
Not to scale

9. A cone and a hemisphere are shown below. The volume of the cone is three times the volume of the hemisphere. To the nearest whole number, what is the radius of the hemisphere in millimetres?

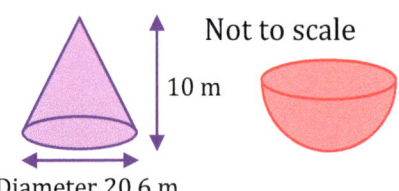
Not to scale

Down

1. How many edges does a cube have?
3. The volume of the cone is 20% the volume of the cylinder. To the nearest whole number, what is the height (x) of the cone in millimetres?

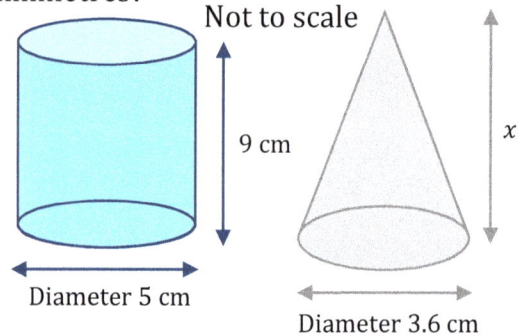
Not to scale

4. Find the surface area of the cylinder in clue 3 down in cm². Multiply the answer by 4.5, round the result to the nearest whole number and write the rounded value in the grid
5. Find the total surface area of the cone in clue 3 down in cm². Multiply the answer by 10.5, round the result to the nearest whole number and write the rounded value in the grid
6. A prism is shown below with $h = 2$ cm, $a = 2$ cm and $b = 4.6$ cm. To the nearest whole number, what is the volume of the prism in cm³?

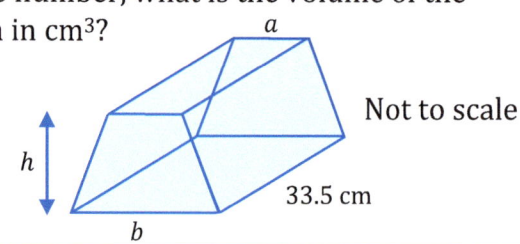
Not to scale

Page | 55

Across continued

12. The square-based pyramid below has a volume of 3667 cm³ and a height of 30 cm. To the nearest whole number, what is the perimeter of its square base in mm?

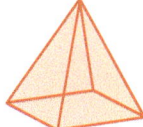

14. The radius of the sphere below is 1.1 cm. To the nearest whole number, what is the surface area of the sphere in cm²?

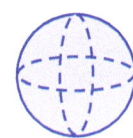

15. Determine the volume of the sphere in clue 14 across in cm³. Multiply the answer by 4 and round the result to the nearest whole number
16. To the nearest whole number, what is the surface area of a sphere with diameter 9.44 cm? Give your answer in cm²
17. How many edges does a pentagonal prism have?

Down continued

8. Each face on the cube below has a perimeter of 10 cm. What is the volume of the cube in mm³?

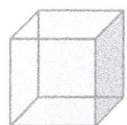

10. The solid below consists of a hemisphere sitting on top of a cylinder. The hemisphere and the cylinder both have a radius of 2 cm. To the nearest whole number, what is the total volume of the solid in cm³?

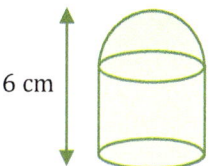

6 cm   Not to scale

11. Find the surface area of the cube in clue 8 down in cm². Multiply the answer by 10 and write the result in the grid
13. How many vertices does a hexagonal prism have?
14. How many faces does an octagonal prism have?

3D Shapes

The number of faces, vertices and edges on some common 3D shapes are shown in the table below:

	Cube/Cuboid	Tetrahedron	Square-based pyramid	Triangular prism	Pentagonal prism	Hexagonal prism	Octagonal prism
Faces	6	4	5	5	7	8	10
Vertices	8	4	5	6	10	12	16
Edges	12	6	8	9	15	18	24

Surface Area and Volume

The formulas for the surface area (A) and volume (V) of some common 3D shapes are shown below:

Cube	Cuboid	Cone	Cylinder	Sphere	Square-based pyramid
$A = 6a^2$ $V = a^3$	$A = 2(hl + bh + bl)$ $V = lbh$	$A = \pi r^2 + \pi r l$ $V = \frac{1}{3}\pi r^2 h$	$A = 2\pi r^2 + 2\pi r h$ $V = \pi r^2 h$	$A = 4\pi r^2$ $V = \frac{4}{3}\pi r^3$	$V = \frac{1}{3}a^2 h$

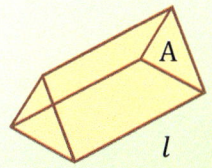

Volume of prism = Area of end face A × length

Crossword 22: Chapter 4 Consolidation Crossword

Note: assume that values k and n are always integers in this crossword

Across

1. A regular pentagon is shown inside a regular octagon below. Both shapes have equal side lengths. Find the size of angle x. Multiply the value of x by 45 and write the result in the grid

   Not to scale

4. Lines AB and CD are parallel. Sum the values of angles c and e and write the result in the grid

   Not to scale

7. $OABC$ is a quadrilateral. D is the midpoint of AB and E is the point on BC such that $BE:EC = 3:2$. $\vec{OA} = 31\mathbf{a}$, $\vec{CB} = 35\mathbf{a}$ and $\vec{OC} = 50\mathbf{b}$. Find $\vec{AB}$ in the form $k\mathbf{a} + n\mathbf{b}$. Write the result of kn in the grid

   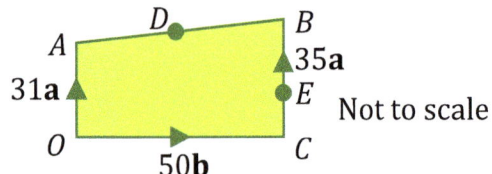
   Not to scale

Down

2. A regular hexagon and a rectangle are shown below. Find the size of angle a. Multiply the value of a by 967 and write the result in the grid

   Not to scale

3. A triangle is shown inside a parallelogram below. The area of the triangle is 3361 cm². To the nearest whole number, what is the area of the shaded region in cm²?

   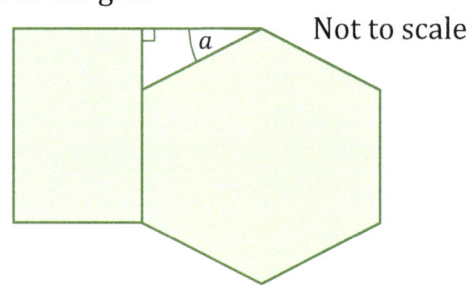
   Not to scale

4. What is the combined number of vertices on 210 triangular prisms and 155 square-based pyramids?

5. To the nearest whole number, what is the perimeter in centimetres of the triangle in clue 3 down?

Across continued

8. Using the diagram in clue 7 across, find $\overrightarrow{DC}$ in the form $k\mathbf{a} + n\mathbf{b}$. Then find the value of $8.5(n - k)$ and write the result in the grid
9. Using the diagram in clue 7 across, find $\overrightarrow{ED}$ in the form $k\mathbf{a} + n\mathbf{b}$. Then find the value of $10k$ and write the result in the grid
10. The area of a circle is 82 cm². To the nearest whole number, what is the radius of the circle in millimetres?
12. The diagram shows a sector of a circle which has a radius of 7.3 centimetres. To the nearest whole number, what is the area of sector XYZ in cm²?

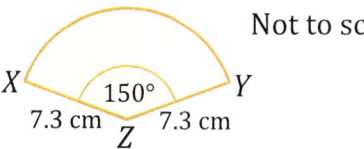

Not to scale

14. To the nearest whole number, what is the length of arc XY in centimetres in clue 12 across?
15. The diagram shows a sector of a circle. The length of arc HI is 4.5 metres, what is the area of the shaded segment in cm² correct to 4 significant figures?

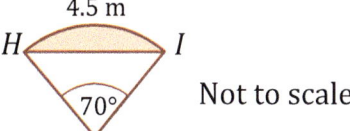

Not to scale

16. A circle with centre O is shown below. Line CTD is a tangent to the circle. Angle $BTD = 69°$ and angle $ABT = 57°$. Find the size of angle b. Multiply the value of angle b by 16 and write the result in the grid

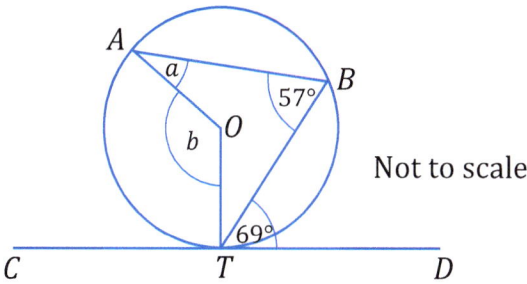

Not to scale

18. Find the size of angle a in the diagram above. Multiply the value of angle a by 1.5 and write the result in the grid
20. To the nearest whole number, calculate the length in millimetres of side y on the right-angled triangle below

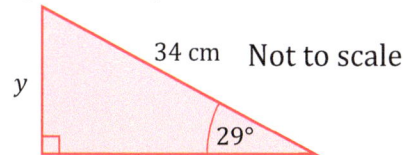

Not to scale

Down continued

6. Translate shape P by the vector $\begin{pmatrix} -3 \\ -2 \end{pmatrix}$ and label it as shape Q on the diagram below. Multiply the largest y-coordinate on the perimeter of shape Q by 63

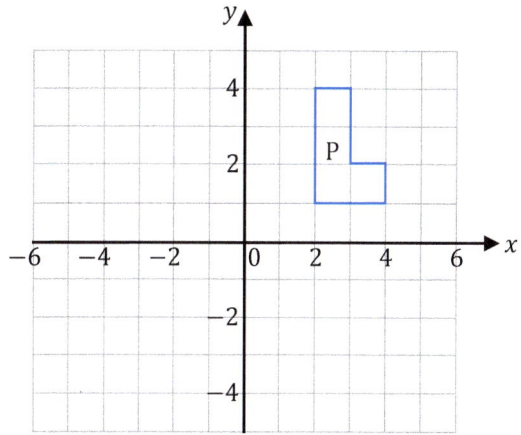

11. On the diagram above, rotate shape P 90° clockwise about $(1, 0)$ and label it shape R. Multiply the largest x-coordinate on the perimeter of shape R by 221
12. On the diagram above, reflect shape P in the line $x = 4$ and label it shape S. Multiply the largest x-coordinate on the perimeter of shape S by 118
13. To the nearest whole number, calculate the length in millimetres of side x on the triangle below

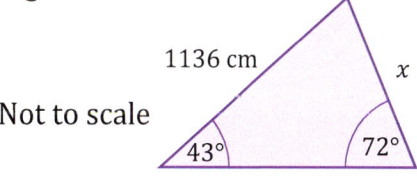

Not to scale

15. A square of area 9.9 cm² is inside the circle below. To the nearest whole number, what is the circumference of the circle in cm?

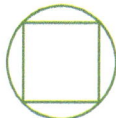

16. The diameter of a sphere is 7.5 cm. To the nearest whole number, what is the surface area of the sphere in cm²?
17. To the nearest integer, what is the volume in cm³ of the sphere in clue 16 down?
19. The radius of a cone is 6.2 cm and its height is 12 cm. To the nearest whole number, what is the volume of the cone in cm³?
20. How many edges does a hexagonal prism have?
21. How many faces in total are on 14 tetrahedrons?

Chapter 5
Probability and Statistics

Crossword 23: Probability

Note: unless stated, probabilities should be calculated as decimals in this crossword

Across

2. The probabilities of Mike and Zoya passing a music test at the first and second attempts are shown in the table below.

	Probability of passing test at	
	attempt one	attempt two
Mike	0.74	0.8
Zoya	0.68	0.85

   What is the probability that Mike and Zoya will both fail the test at the first attempt? Multiply the answer by 10000 and write the result in the grid

5. Using the table in clue 2 across, calculate the probability of Mike passing the test within the first two attempts. Multiply the answer by 301, round the result to the nearest whole number and write the rounded value in the grid

7. For the music test mentioned above, the average chance of anyone passing the test at the first attempt is 0.72. If 4000 people take the test for the first time, how many are likely to pass?

10. A box contains only black and blue pens. The probability of randomly selecting a blue pen is $\frac{3}{4}$. After removing 6 blue pens from the box, the probability of selecting a blue pen becomes $\frac{5}{7}$. Determine the total number of pens originally in the box. If one of the pens is faulty, how many pens are working? Enter this number in the grid

Down

1. The probability that Derek is late for work on Thursday is 0.3. If he is late on Thursday, the probability he is late on Friday is 0.5. If he is on time on Thursday, the probability he is late on Friday is 0.4. Complete the tree diagram below to represent this information.

   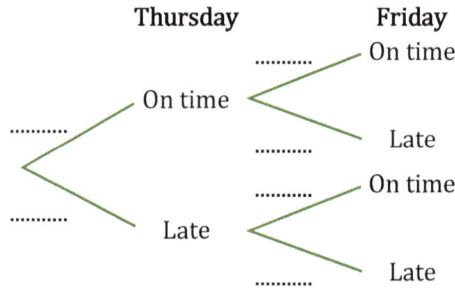

   What is the probability that Derek arrives at work on time on both Thursday and Friday? Give your answer as a percentage

2. Using the information in clue 1 down, calculate the probability that Derek arrives at work on time on at least one of the two days. Give your answer as a percentage

3. Using the information in clue 1 down, calculate the probability (as a percentage) that Derek arrives late for work on exactly one of the two days. Multiply the answer by 6 and write the result in the grid

4. 6 red boxes and x green boxes are stored in an empty warehouse. 2 boxes are removed at random from the warehouse without replacement. The probability that the 2 boxes are green is $\frac{2}{15}$. Find x and write the value of $30x$ in the grid

Across continued

11. A fair six-sided dice with integers 1 to 6 on it and a fair four-sided spinner with numbers 1 to 4 on it are rolled and spun at the same time. The product of the two numbers are recorded and some of the results are shown in the sample space table below.

		\multicolumn{6}{c}{Dice outcome}
		1	2	3	4	5	6
Spinner outcome	1	1	2				6
	2					10	
	3		6		12		18
	4	4				20	

Complete the sample space table. Calculate the probability (as a fraction) of recording a product of at least 9. Multiply the answer by 600 and write the result in the grid

12. A Venn diagram is shown below.

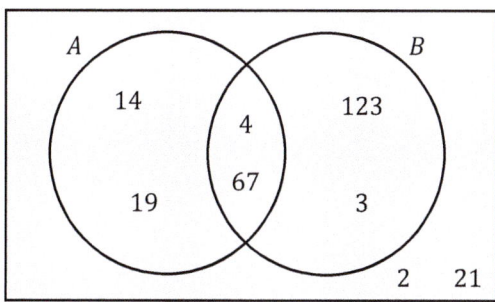

What is the product of all the numbers that are in set $A \cap B$?

13. Using the information in clue 12 across, what is the sum of all the numbers that are in set B'?

14. Using the information in clue 12 across, find $P(A \cup B)$. Multiply the answer by 1000 and write the result in the grid

Down continued

6. A box contains paper clips that are small, medium and large. The table below shows the probability of selecting each size of paper clip.

	Small	Medium	Large
Probability	$1.25x$	$4x$	x

A paper clip is selected from the box at random. What is the probability (as a percentage) that it is not large?

7. Using the information in clue 4 down, what is the probability (as a percentage to the nearest whole number) that the first box selected from the warehouse is red and the second is green?

8. Using the information in clue 6 down, if there were 1275 paper clips in the box, how many would you expect to be medium?

9. 100 people were asked if they liked apples, bananas and oranges. All 100 people responded and liked at least 1 of the 3 fruits. 46 people liked all 3 fruits, 16 liked apples and oranges but did not like bananas, 66 liked bananas and oranges, 52 liked apples and bananas, 73 liked apples and 86 liked oranges. Produce a Venn diagram to show this information. Determine the probability (as a percentage) that a person chosen from the 100 at random likes bananas. Multiply the answer by 17 and write the result in the grid

10. Using the information in clue 9 down, determine the probability (as a percentage) that a person chosen at random from the 100 likes only 1 of the 3 fruits. Multiply the answer by 34 and write the result in the grid

12. The probability that any light bulb is faulty is $\frac{1}{6}$. Of 354 light bulbs, how many are likely to be working correctly?

Venn Diagrams

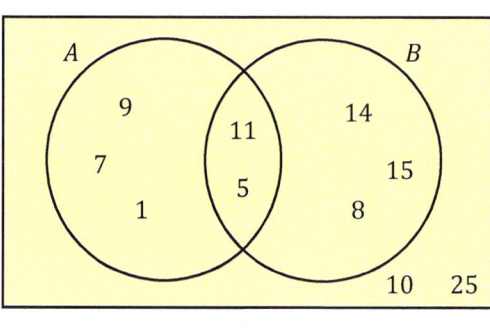

Numbers in set $A = 1, 5, 7, 9, 11$.
Numbers in set $B = 5, 8, 11, 14, 15$.
Numbers in set $A' = 8, 10, 14, 15, 25$. (A' means not in set A)
Numbers in set $A \cap B = 5, 11$.   ($A \cap B$ means A and B)
Numbers in set $A \cup B = 1, 5, 7, 8, 9, 11, 14, 15$.
    ($A \cup B$ means A or B)

$P(A) = \frac{5}{10} = \frac{1}{2}$, $P(B) = \frac{5}{10} = \frac{1}{2}$.
$P(A \cap B) = \frac{2}{10} = \frac{1}{5}$.
$P(A \cup B) = P(A) + P(B) - P(A \cap B) = \frac{1}{2} + \frac{1}{2} - \frac{1}{5} = \frac{4}{5}$

Crossword 24: Statistics

Across

1. Laura played a computer game 12 times. She completed the game in the following times (all in minutes):
   22, 18, 40, 14, 28, 23, 25, 39, 22, 28, 19, 22.
   Calculate the mean time (in minutes) that it took Laura to complete the game
2. Using the information in clue 1 across, find the mode time (in minutes) that it took Laura to complete the game
4. Using the information in clue 1 across, calculate the range in times (in minutes) that it took Laura to complete the game
5. The table below shows summary information for the number of CDs owned by a group of people. Two of the frequencies are missing and are written as expressions involving an integer c. The mean number of CDs owned per person is estimated to be 8. How many people in total are in the group?

Number of CDs	Number of people (f)	Midpoint (x)	fx
0 to 2	13	1	
3 to 7	$3c+1$	5	
8 to 12	$5c-4$	10	
13 to 19	12	16	
Totals:			

6. Using the box plot below, determine the range of test marks in the dataset

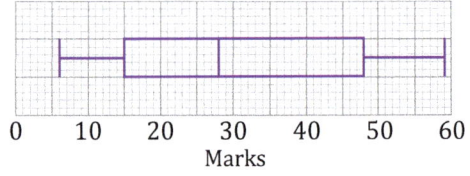

Down

1. The table below shows summary information on the age groups of 80 people. Complete the table and find an estimate for the mean age in years. Multiply the answer by 9.5 and write the result in the grid

Age group (a) years	Number of people (f)	Midpoint (x)	fx
$10 \leq a < 20$	15		
$20 \leq a < 30$	26	25	
$30 \leq a < 40$	23		805
$40 \leq a < 50$	16		
Totals:	80		

2. Using the information in clue 1 down, determine the modal class interval in the form $m \leq a < n$ where m and n are integers. Multiply the value of m by 134.5 and write the result in the grid
3. Using the information in clue 1 across, calculate the median time (in minutes to the nearest 10 minutes) that it took Laura to complete the game
5. The number of hours walked on a Sunday by 7 people are as follows:
   5.7, 3.2, 4.0, 0.5, 5.3, 1.7, 0.3.
   Draw a box plot on the diagram below for this information. Subtract the median time in minutes from 941 minutes and write the result in the grid

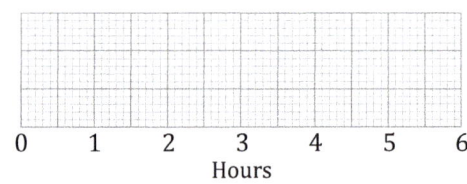

Across continued

8. Using the information in clue 6 across, determine the median and interquartile range (IQR) of the marks. Find the product of the median and IQR values and write the result in the grid
9. The histogram shows information about the weights of all members of a club. 16 members of the club weigh between 50 and 60 kilograms. Work out the total number of members in the club

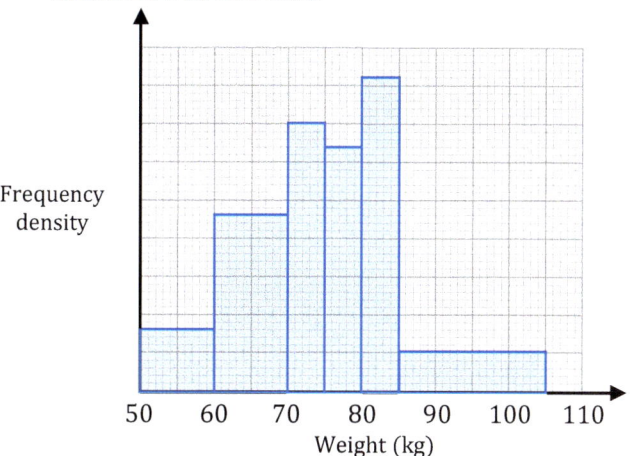

10. Using the information in clue 9 across, how many members weigh 75 kg or more?
12. Using the information in clue 9 across, estimate the number of club members weighing between 65 kg and 75 kg
14. There are 30000 members of a gym. A sample of 200 members were asked what their favourite sport was. 45 said football, 35 said netball, 116 said running and 4 said weightlifting. Use this information to give an estimate for the total number of members whose favourite sport is running

Down continued

7. Using the information in clue 5 down, write the upper quartile value (in minutes) in the grid
11. The cumulative frequency graph shows the marks achieved in a test by 200 students. Find the upper quartile mark. Multiply the value by 100 and write the result in the grid

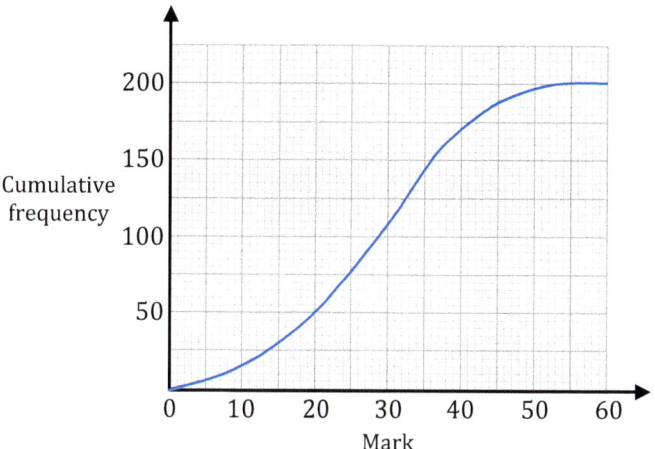

12. Using the information in clue 11 down, find the median mark. Multiply the value by 20 and write the result in the grid
13. Consider the information in clue 11 down. The lowest performing 15% of students on the test are selected for additional revision sessions. Use the graph to estimate the highest mark achieved by the bottom 15% of students. Multiply this value by 23 and write the result in the grid
14. Using the information in clue 11 down, find the interquartile range of the marks

Statistics

A dataset consists of the values 0, −2, 3, 5, 3, 9, −3, 0, 3.

Mean = $\frac{\text{sum of values}}{\text{amount of values}} = \frac{0 + (-2) + 3 + 5 + 3 + 9 + (-3) + 0 + 3}{9} = \frac{18}{9} = 2$.

Mode = the most frequently occurring value = 3 (3 times).
Range = highest value − lowest value = 9 − (−3) = 12.
Median (Q2) = middle value of ascendingly ordered dataset.
Dataset in ascending order: −3, −2, 0, 0, 3, 3, 3, 5, 9.
Q2 occurs at the $\frac{1}{2}(n + 1)$th value = $\frac{1}{2}(9 + 1)$th = 5th value.
Q2 = 3 as the value 3 is in the 5th position.
Lower quartile (Q1) occurs 25% of the way through the dataset.
Upper quartile (Q3) occurs 75% of the way through the dataset

Interval	Frequency (f)	Midpoint (x)	fx
0 to 10	20	5	100
11 to 17	10	14	140
18 to 22	20	20	400
Totals:	50		640

Grouped Data

Mean = $\frac{\sum fx}{\sum f} = \frac{640}{50} = 12.8$

Histograms
The y-axis in a histogram is the frequency density, where:

Frequency density = $\frac{\text{frequency}}{\text{class width}}$

Box plots

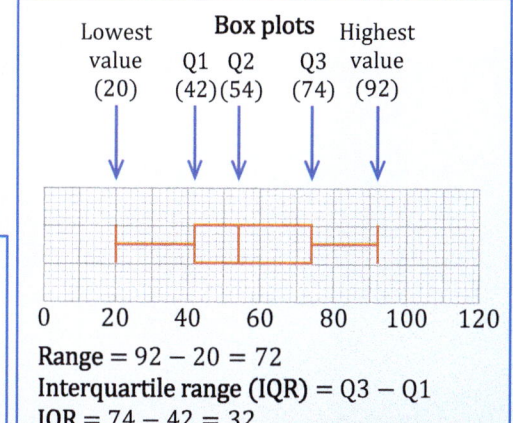

Range = 92 − 20 = 72
Interquartile range (IQR) = Q3 − Q1
IQR = 74 − 42 = 32

Crossword 25: Chapter 5 Consolidation Crossword

Note: unless stated, probabilities should be calculated as decimals in this crossword

Across

1. Juan tries to catch the 5pm bus home every evening. The table below shows the likelihood of the bus having a number of vacant seats when Juan first gets on. Assuming the probabilities are true for all days of the week, what is the probability that the bus will have 2 or more vacant seats on a Monday? Give your answer as a percentage

Number of vacant seats	0	1	2	3	4 or more
Probability	0.35	0.13	0.09	0.27	0.16

3. Using the information in clue 1 across, determine the probability (as a percentage to the nearest whole number) that the sum of the number of vacant seats over two consecutive days is exactly 3
5. A fair six-sided dice with integers 1 to 6 on it is to be rolled three times. Find the probability (as a fraction) that the dice lands face up on one odd number and two even numbers, in any order. Multiply the answer by 2336 and write the result in the grid
7. Using the information in clue 5 across, find the probability (as a fraction) that the dice lands face up on at least two even numbers. Multiply the answer by 186 and write the result in the grid

Down

2. The probability of a person having green eyes is $\frac{1}{6}$ and the probability of a person having brown eyes is $\frac{2}{7}$. Two people are chosen at random. Calculate the probability (as a fraction) that one person will have green eyes and the other will have brown eyes. Multiply the answer by 304500 and write the result in the grid
4. Using the information in clue 2 down, calculate the probability (as a fraction in its simplest terms) that both people will have brown eyes. Multiply the numerator and denominator values of the answer together and write the result in the grid
5. Lian has 30 small pieces of card in her pocket made up of the following colours:

Orange	Green	Purple
16 cards	6 cards	8 cards

   She takes out two cards at random from her pocket. Calculate the probability (as a fraction) that the two cards are of the same colour. Multiply the answer by 2175 and write the result in the grid
6. The probability of any train being late is $\frac{1}{12}$. Of 6696 trains, how many are likely to be on time?

Across continued

8. The universal set (ξ) is as follows:
$\xi = \{1, 2, 4, 5, 6, 8, 9, 10, 12, 13\}$,
O = odd numbers,
P = prime numbers.
Complete the Venn diagram below. Find the sum of all the numbers that are in set P' and write the result in the grid

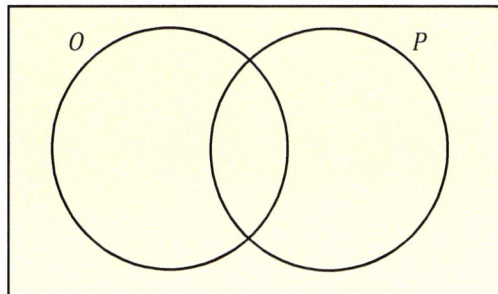

9. Consider the diagram in clue 8 across. Given that a member selected at random from the universal set is odd, find the probability that the member is also prime. Multiply the answer by 13350 and write the result in the grid
10. Find the sum of all the numbers that are in set $O \cap P$ for the data in clue 8 across
11. Using the box plot below, multiply the median age (in years) by 179 and write the result in the grid

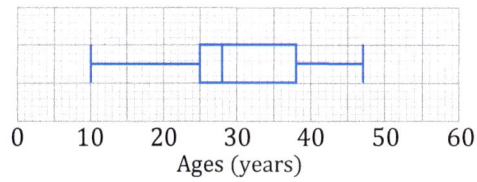

13. Using the box plot above, multiply the interquartile range by 15 and write the result in the grid
14. Using the box plot above, what is the lower quartile value in years?
16. Using the box plot above, determine the range of ages in years in the dataset
17. In a histogram, the class width of a bar is 9 and the frequency density is 6. What frequency does this represent?
19. In a histogram, the class width of a bar is 26 and the frequency density is 24. What frequency does this represent?
20. What is the median of the following 5 numbers? 450, 340, 500, 500, 250
21. What is the mean of the following 6 numbers? 240, 218, 180, 167, 290, 273

Down continued

9. The probability that it rains on Tuesday is 0.9. If it rains on Tuesday, the probability it rains on Wednesday is 0.98. If it does not rain on Tuesday, the probability that it rains on Wednesday is 0.6. Complete the tree diagram.

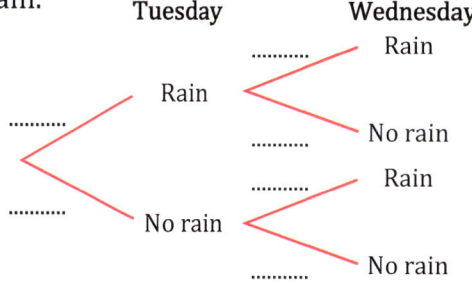

What is the probability that it rains on at least one day? Multiply the answer by 700 and write the result in the grid

10. Some blue marbles and x red marbles are placed in an empty box in the ratio 3 : 1. 2 marbles are removed at random from the box without replacement. The probability that the 2 marbles are red is $\frac{7}{118}$. Find x and write the value of $103x$ in the grid
12. The table below shows information on the weekly rainfall in a town. Complete the table and find an estimate for the mean weekly rainfall in mm. Multiply the answer by 374 and write the result in the grid

Weekly rainfall (r) in mm	Number of weeks (f)	Midpoint (x)	fx
$0 \leq r < 16$	5		
$16 \leq r < 24$	12		240
$24 \leq r < 40$	25	32	
$40 \leq r < 60$	18		
Totals:	60		

13. Using the information in clue 12 down, find the probability (as a fraction) that a randomly selected week had at least 24 mm of rain. Multiply the answer by 2100 and write the result in the grid
15. Using the information in clue 12 down, determine the modal class interval in the form $m \leq r < n$ where m and n are integers. Write the value of $m \times n$ in the grid
18. Using the information in clue 12 down, determine the class interval that the lower quartile resides in. Give the interval in the form $b \leq r < c$ where b and c are integers. Write the value of $28b$ in the grid
20. There are 600 boys and 400 girls at a school. A stratified sample of 120 is taken. How many girls should be included in the sample?

Crossword Solutions

Crossword 1

	1	2		3	4
	2	7		2	4	5
5		6			
4		6	3			0
7	8			9	
1	1	5		8	7	0
			10		
	4		2	2		
11		12			13
9	7	1	7		1
				14	
	9		9	1	2	7
15					
	6	0	8	0	0	5

Across

1. $-8 + (-17) - (-52) = -8 - 17 + 52 = 27$
3. $\frac{7^2 \times (3+7)}{8 - (\sqrt{9} \times 2)} = \frac{49 \times 10}{8 - (3 \times 2)} = \frac{490}{2} = 245$
6. Left-hand side: $-5 + 12 = 7$ is $<$ right-hand side: $27 \div 3 = 9$. Value underneath $<$ is 63
7. Left-hand side: $-4 - 15 = -19$ is $\neq$ right-hand side: $-6 + 1 = -5$. Value underneath $\neq$ is 115
9. $29 \times 30 = 870$
10. $17°C - (-5°C) = 17°C + 5°C = 22°C$
11. $9.717 \times 10^3 = 9717$
14. $(1.105 \times 10^3) - (9.78 \times 10^2) = 1105 - 978 = 127$
15. $(3.04 \times 10^3) \div (5 \times 10^{-2}) = 3040 \div 0.05 = 60800$

Down

2. $(-5 \times 51) \times (-7 - (-4)) = (-255) \times (-7 + 4) = (-255) \times (-3) = 765$
4. $\frac{1}{0.002} = 500$
5. Left-hand side: $-3 \times -5 \times 2 = 30$ is $\leq$ right-hand side: $14 + 3 - (-13) = 17 + 13 = 30$. Value underneath $\leq$ is 41
8. £2940000 ÷ 20000 = £147
9. Number of draws = $30 - (11 + 11) = 8$. Number of points = $(11 \times 6) + (8 \times 2) = 82$
10. As $0.12 \times 2.25 = 0.27$, 1.2×22.5 must be 27 as $1 \times 22.5 = 22.5$, which is close to 27
11. As $400 \times 249 = 99600$, 40×24.9 must be 996 as $40 \times 25 = 1000$, which is close to 996
12. As $4400 \times 45 = 198000$, 44×4.5 must be 198 as $44 \times 5 = 220$, which is close to 198
13. Length = (3.5×10^4) mm = 35000 mm = 35 m. Width = $35 \div 7 = 5$ m. Area = $35 \times 5 = 175$ m²
14. $81{,}432{,}156{,}302 = 8.1432156302 \times 10^{10}$. Therefore, $n = 10$

Crossword 2

1		2		3	4	
1	6	8	■	1	2	5
0	■	5 / 4	6 / 5	■	0	■
7 / 8	8 / 1	■	9 / 9	9	0	■
■	10 / 8	5	8	■	■	11 / 2
12 / 3	0	■	13 / 4	14 / 8	■	1
6	■	15 / 8	■	16 / 3	3	6
0	■	17 / 4	0	0	■	0

Across
1. $7 \times 24 = 168$
3. $80 = 2 \times 2 \times 2 \times 2 \times 5 = 2^4 \times 5$. Therefore, $5 \times 25 = 125$
5. $96 = 2 \times 2 \times 2 \times 2 \times 2 \times 3 = 2^5 \times 3$. Therefore, $n = 5, 5 \times 9 = 45$
7. $42 = 2 \times 3 \times 7$ and $56 = 2 \times 2 \times 2 \times 7$. HCF = product of shared prime factors $= 2 \times 7 = 14$. Therefore, $14 + 67 = 81$
9. HCF = product of shared prime factors $= 2 \times 3 = 6$. LCM = product of HCF and remaining prime factors $= 6 \times 3 \times 5 = 90$. Therefore, $90 \times 11 = 990$
10. $78 = 2 \times 3 \times 13$ and $286 = 2 \times 11 \times 13$. HCF $= 2 \times 13 = 26$. LCM $= 26 \times 3 \times 11 = 858$
12. $x = 2^3 \times 3 \times 5^2$, $y = \frac{3}{4}x = \frac{3}{2^2}(2^3 \times 3 \times 5^2) = 2 \times 3^2 \times 5^2$ and $z = \frac{x}{10} = \frac{1}{(2 \times 5)}(2^3 \times 3 \times 5^2) = 2^2 \times 3 \times 5$. HCF $= 2 \times 3 \times 5 = 30$
13. Factors of 768 are 1, 2, 3, 4, 6, 8, 12, 16, 24, 32, 48, 64, 96, 128, 192, 256, 384 and 768. Of these factors, 24, 32, 48, 64 are between 20 and 95. Only 48 is a multiple of 16 and 24
16. There are 8 options for the 1st toy he gives to Marilyn, 7 options for the 2nd toy he gives to Frank and 6 options for the 3rd toy he gives to David. There are $8 \times 7 \times 6 = 336$ different options
17. There are 8 options for the 1st digit (2 to 9), 10 options for the 2nd digit (0 to 9) and 5 options for the 3rd digit (0, 2, 4, 6 or 8). Therefore, there are $8 \times 10 \times 5 = 400$ different numbers

Down
1. Factors of 85: 1, 5, 17, 85. Therefore, $1 + 5 + 17 + 85 = 108$
2. Factors of 44: 1, 2, 4, 11, 22, 44. Therefore, $1 + 2 + 4 + 11 + 22 + 44 = 84$
4. Values in empty circles: $5 \times 5 = 25$, $2 \times 25 = 50$, $2 \times 50 = 100$ and $2 \times 100 = 200 = x$
6. $66 = 2 \times 3 \times 11$ and $110 = 2 \times 5 \times 11$. HCF $= 2 \times 11 = 22$. Therefore, $22 \times 272 = 5984$
8. $20 = 2 \times 2 \times 5$ and $36 = 2 \times 2 \times 3 \times 3$. HCF $= 2 \times 2 = 4$. LCM = product of HCF and remaining prime factors $= 4 \times 3 \times 3 \times 5 = 180$
11. $9 = 3 \times 3$ and $12 = 2 \times 2 \times 3$. HCF $= 3$. LCM $= 3 \times 3 \times 2 \times 2 = 36$. They will both next sip some water at the same time 36 minutes after 10 am. 36 minutes $= 36 \times 60 = 2160$ seconds
12. Multiples of 15 between 300 and 400 are 300, 315, 330, 345, 360, 375 and 390. Of these, 360 is the only value which is exactly divisible by 8
14. Total outfits $= 2 \times 5 \times 83 = 830$
15. Option 1: DVD and CD, $3 \times 4 = 12$. Option 2: DVD, CD and a book, $3 \times 4 \times 6 = 72$. Total options: $12 + 72 = 84$

Crossword 3

	1			2		3	
1	1	2	■	6	1	6	■
	5	■	4	5	■	2	■
	5			■	6		7
	4	9	0	■	6	4	5
	■	■	■	8		■	
	■	■	■	2	3	■	4
	9	10			■	11	■
	3	1	2	5	■	3	■
	■		■	12	13		14
	■	1	■	6	7	2	7
	15			■		■	
	2	7	0	■	6	■	5

Across

1. $\sqrt{a} \times \sqrt{b} = \sqrt{ab}$. Therefore, $\sqrt{8} \times \sqrt{18} = \sqrt{144} = 12$
2. $(14 - \sqrt{7})(6 + \sqrt{7}) = 84 + 14\sqrt{7} - 6\sqrt{7} - \sqrt{7}\sqrt{7} = 84 + 8\sqrt{7} - 7 = 77 + 8\sqrt{7}$. Therefore, $a = 77, b = 8$. $a \times b = 77 \times 8 = 616$
4. $\sqrt{128} = \sqrt{64 \times 2} = \sqrt{64} \times \sqrt{2} = 8\sqrt{2}$. Therefore, $a = 8$. $47 + a = 47 + 8 = 55$
5. As $\frac{\sqrt{a}}{\sqrt{b}} = \sqrt{\frac{a}{b}}, \frac{\sqrt{180}}{\sqrt{5}} = \sqrt{\frac{180}{5}} = \sqrt{36} = 6$. Therefore, $496 - 6 = 490$
6. Using Pythagoras' Theorem, $x = \sqrt{13^2 + 9^2} = \sqrt{250} = \sqrt{2}\sqrt{5}\sqrt{25} = 5\sqrt{2}\sqrt{5}$ cm. Therefore, $a = 5$. $a \times 129 = 5 \times 129 = 645$
8. $(5^7 \div 5^5) - (2 \times 5^0) = (5^{7-5}) - (2 \times 1) = 5^2 - 2 = 25 - 2 = 23$
9. $25^{2\frac{1}{2}} = 25^{\frac{5}{2}} = (\sqrt{25})^5 = 5^5 = 3125$
12. $196^{\frac{1}{2}} \times 4^{-\frac{1}{2}} \times 31^2 = \sqrt{196} \times \frac{1}{\sqrt{4}} \times 961 = 14 \times \frac{1}{2} \times 961 = 6727$
15. $2x^3y \times 5y^2 = 10x^3y^3 = 10(1)^3(3)^3 = 270$

Down

1. $\frac{2+\sqrt{8}}{3-\sqrt{8}} \times \frac{3+\sqrt{8}}{3+\sqrt{8}} = \frac{(2+\sqrt{8})(3+\sqrt{8})}{(3-\sqrt{8})(3+\sqrt{8})} = \frac{6 + 2\sqrt{8} + 3\sqrt{8} + \sqrt{8}\sqrt{8}}{9 + 3\sqrt{8} - 3\sqrt{8} - \sqrt{8}\sqrt{8}} = \frac{6 + 5\sqrt{8} + 8}{9 - 8} = 14 + 5\sqrt{2}\sqrt{4} = 14 + 10\sqrt{2}$. Therefore, $a = 14$. $a \times 11 = 14 \times 11 = 154$
2. As $(\sqrt{a})^2 = a$, $5 \times (\sqrt{13})^2 = 5 \times 13 = 65$
3. $\frac{72}{\sqrt{3}} \times \frac{\sqrt{3}}{\sqrt{3}} = \frac{72\sqrt{3}}{3} = 24\sqrt{3}$. Therefore, $a = 24$. $a \times 26 = 24 \times 26 = 624$
4. Area $= \sqrt{5}(\sqrt{20} + \sqrt{10}) = \sqrt{5}(\sqrt{4}\sqrt{5} + \sqrt{2}\sqrt{5}) = 2\sqrt{5}\sqrt{5} + \sqrt{5}\sqrt{5}\sqrt{2} = (10 + 5\sqrt{2})$ cm². Therefore, $a = 10, b = 5$. $a \times b = 10 \times 5 = 50$
6. Perimeter $= 2(\sqrt{5}) + 2(\sqrt{20} + \sqrt{10}) = 2\sqrt{5} + 2\sqrt{20} + 2\sqrt{10} = 2\sqrt{5} + 2\sqrt{4}\sqrt{5} + 2\sqrt{2}\sqrt{5}$
   $= 2\sqrt{5} + 4\sqrt{5} + 2\sqrt{2}\sqrt{5} = 6\sqrt{5} + 2\sqrt{2}\sqrt{5} = 2\sqrt{5}(3 + \sqrt{2})$ cm. $a = 3$. $a \times 21 = 3 \times 21 = 63$
7. $3^{-2} = \frac{1}{3^2} = \frac{1}{9}$. Therefore, $\frac{1}{9} \times 486 = 54$
8. $(u^2)^4 = u^{2 \times 4} = u^8 = 2^8 = 256$
10. $9^2 + 216^{\frac{2}{3}} = 81 + (\sqrt[3]{216})^2 = 81 + 36 = 117$
11. $2^7 \times 16^{-\frac{1}{2}} = 128 \times \frac{1}{\sqrt{16}} = 32$
13. $(6\frac{1}{4})^{-\frac{1}{2}} \times 190 = (\frac{25}{4})^{-\frac{1}{2}} \times 190 = (\frac{4}{25})^{\frac{1}{2}} \times 190 = \frac{\sqrt{4}}{\sqrt{25}} \times 190 = \frac{2}{5} \times 190 = 76$
14. $\frac{3x^4y^2 \times 8xy}{4x^3y^2} = \frac{24x^5y^3}{4x^3y^2} = 6x^2y = 6(5)^2(0.5) = 75$

Crossword 4

Across

1. $\frac{7}{8}, \frac{49}{4}, \frac{15}{2}, \frac{12}{8}, \frac{3}{4}, \frac{4}{4}$ are equivalent to $\frac{7}{8}, \frac{98}{8}, \frac{60}{8}, \frac{12}{8}, \frac{6}{8}, \frac{8}{8}$. Ascending order: $\frac{3}{4}, \frac{7}{8}, \frac{4}{4}, \frac{12}{8}, \frac{15}{2}, \frac{49}{4}$. $\frac{98}{8} + \frac{6}{8} = 13$
3. $x = \frac{(6 \times 45)}{5} = 54$
4. $6 \times 4\frac{2}{5} \times 1\frac{2}{3} = \frac{6}{1} \times \frac{22}{5} \times \frac{5}{3} = \frac{(6 \times 22 \times 5)}{(1 \times 5 \times 3)} = \frac{660}{15} = 44$
5. Let $x = 0.405405405..$ Therefore, $1000x - x = 405.405405.. - 0.405405..$ This simplifies to $999x = 405$, which implies that $x = \frac{405}{999} = \frac{15}{37}$. Denominator $= 37$
7. $\frac{3.6 \times (14.75 - (-19.5))}{0.018} = \frac{3.6 \times (14.75 + 19.5)}{0.018} = \frac{3.6 \times 34.25}{0.018} = \frac{123.3}{0.018} = 6850$
9. Let $x = 0.863636363..$ Therefore, $1000x - 10x = 863.636363.. - 8.636363..$ This simplifies to $990x = 855$, which implies that $x = \frac{855}{990} = \frac{19}{22}$. Numerator $= 19$
10. Let $x = 0.39393939..$ Therefore, $100x - x = 39.393939.. - 0.393939..$ This simplifies to $99x = 39$, which implies that $x = \frac{39}{99} = \frac{13}{33}$. Denominator $= 33$
11. $\left(6\frac{3}{10} + 2\frac{4}{5}\right) \div \frac{1}{70} = \left(\frac{63}{10} + \frac{14}{5}\right) \div \frac{1}{70} = \left(\frac{63}{10} + \frac{28}{10}\right) \div \frac{1}{70} = \frac{91}{10} \times \frac{70}{1} = 91 \times 7 = 637$
13. New value $= £500 - (£500 \times 0.48) = £500 - £240 = £260$
14. Total price in sale $= \left(\frac{2}{3} \times £420\right) + (0.85 \times £700) = £280 + £595 = £875$
15. Side length of square $= \frac{48}{4} = 12$ cm. Area of square $= 12^2 = 144$ cm². Area of rectangle $= 72 \times 20 = 1440$ cm². % of rectangle shaded $= \frac{1440 - 144}{1440} \times 100 = 90\%$

Down

1. $14\frac{5}{7} = \frac{(14 \times 7) + 5}{7} = \frac{103}{7}$. Denominator $= 7$ and numerator $= 103$
2. Number in year 6 $= \frac{876}{4} = 219$. Number of girls in year 6 $= 219 - \left(\frac{219}{3}\right) = 219 - 73 = 146$
3. Fraction of matches lost $= 1 - \left(\frac{9}{25} + \frac{1}{8}\right) = 1 - \left(\frac{72}{200} + \frac{25}{200}\right) = 1 - \frac{97}{200} = \frac{103}{200}$. Matches lost $= 1000 \times \frac{103}{200} = 515$
6. $\frac{0.8 \times 356.5}{\sqrt{0.16}} = \frac{285.2}{0.4} = 713$
8. Current length $= 6$ m $= 6000$ mm. New length $= 6000 \times 1.36 = 8160$ mm
10. To convert to a decimal, make the denominator 10, 100, 1000 etc. $\frac{41}{125} \times \frac{8}{8} = \frac{328}{1000} = 0.328$. The three digits after the decimal point are 328
12. Original price $\times 0.7 = £553$. Therefore, original price $= \frac{£553}{0.7} = £790$
13. % increase $= \frac{(\text{new price} - \text{old price})}{\text{old price}} \times 100 = \frac{(660p - 528p)}{528p} \times 100 = \frac{132}{528} \times 100 = \frac{1}{4} \times 100 = 25\%$

Crossword 5

	1		2		3	
	1		1	4	4	2
4	3	0	1		1	
8						
	2		5	6		7
			7	5	0	2
	8	9				
	7	9		8	-	4
10				11		
2		9		1	5	
		12				13
6		6	4	0		2
14				15		
5	6	7		8	4	8

Across

2. Weight of 6 chocolate bars = 6 × 45 = 270 g.
   Number of calories in 1 g = 534 ÷ 100 = 5.34 cal.
   Number of calories in 270 g = 270 × 5.34 = 1441.8 cal = 1442 cal to the nearest calorie
4. 8.300724 = 8.301 to 3 decimal places. 8.301 × 1000 = 8301
5. Diameter = 97.736 cm. Radius = 97.736 ÷ 2 = 48.868 cm. Area = $\pi r^2 = \pi \times (48.868)^2$.
   Therefore, area = 7502.37.. cm² = 7502 cm² to 4 significant figures
8. 0.0078519 = 0.0079 to 2 significant figures. 0.0079 × 10000 = 79
11. $\sqrt{4.69 \times (5.24)^2 + 101.94} \approx \sqrt{5 \times (5)^2 + 100} = \sqrt{5 \times 25 + 100} = \sqrt{125 + 100} = \sqrt{225} = 15$
12. $\frac{8.4 \times 42}{0.47} \approx \frac{8 \times 40}{0.5} = \frac{320}{0.5} = 640$
14. $(87.04 - (2.81)^3) \times 8.85 \approx (90 - (3)^3) \times 9 = (90 - 27) \times 9 = 63 \times 9 = 567$
15. $c = \sqrt{(409.55)^2 + (742.65)^2} = 848.09..$ cm = 848 cm to the nearest cm

Down

1. £17.50 is equivalent to 17.5 × 75.84 = 1327.2 rubles, which is 1327 rubles to the nearest ruble
2. Volume of tank = 2.5 × 1.3 × 1.4 = 4.55 m³. Capacity of full tank = 4.55 × 1000 = 4550 litres.
   Amount of water in tank when 90% full = 0.9 × 4550 = 4095 litres. Minutes required for water level in the tank to reach 4095 litres = 4095 ÷ 35 = 117 minutes
3. 409.349 = 410 to 2 significant figures
6. 58108.09999 = 58108 to the nearest whole number
7. 540 = 5.4×10^2. Therefore, $(5.4 \times 10^2) \div (1.8 \times 10^{-22}) = (5.4 \div 1.8) \times (10^2 \div 10^{-22})$
   $= 3 \times 10^{2--22} = 3 \times 10^{2+22} = 3 \times 10^{24} = a \times 10^b$. Hence, b = 24
9. Lower bound of D = product of lower bound of x and lower bound of y.
   D = 55.205 × 180.55 = 9967.26275 = 9967 to the nearest whole number
10. 2.7 rounded to one decimal place has an error interval of 2.65 ≤ n < 2.75. 2.65 × 100 = 265
13. Upper bound of T = upper bound of x divided by lower bound of y.
    $T = \frac{9.5}{0.335} = 28.35.. = 28$ to the nearest whole number

Crossword 6

	1	2		3		4		5
	1	3	2	9		1	5	2
6								
1		2		2		5		7
7				8				
6	8	0		2	1	6		0
2				5		0		0
		9	10		11		12	
0		1	5		6		8	0
	13		14					
	3		2	5	6	7	2	
15		16				17	18	
3	2	9	2			4	9	
					19	20		
8		4			1	8		1
		21				22		
8		5	4	6		2	3	0

Across

1. $-50 \times (-32 + 6) - (-29) = (-50 \times -26) + 29 = 1329$
2. $\frac{76 \times (3-5)^2}{12 - (\sqrt{400} \times 0.5)} = \frac{76 \times (-2)^2}{12 - (20 \times 0.5)} = \frac{76 \times 4}{12 - 10} = \frac{304}{2} = 152$
7. Area of trapezium $= \frac{1}{2}(a+b)h$. $a = (3.1 \times 10^4)$ mm $= 31000$ mm $= 31$ m.
   $b = (3.7 \times 10^4)$ mm $= 37000$ mm $= 37$ m. $h = (2.0 \times 10^3)$ cm $= 2000$ cm $= 20$ m.
   Area $= \frac{1}{2}(31 + 37) \times 20 = 680$ m²
8. Factors of 102: 1, 2, 3, 6, 17, 34, 51, 102. Therefore, $1 + 2 + 3 + 6 + 17 + 34 + 51 + 102 = 216$
9. $75 = 3 \times 5 \times 5$ and $135 = 3 \times 3 \times 3 \times 5$. HCF = product of shared prime factors $= 3 \times 5 = 15$
12. Area $= (2 + \sqrt{5})^2 = (2 + \sqrt{5}) \times (2 + \sqrt{5}) = 4 + 4\sqrt{5} + \sqrt{5}\sqrt{5} = (9 + 4\sqrt{5})$ m².
    Therefore, $a = 9, b = 4$. $b \times 20 = 4 \times 20 = 80$
14. $\frac{120 \times (219.67 + 37.05)}{1.2} = \frac{120 \times 256.72}{1.2} = 25672$
15. Area $= \frac{1}{2} \times 92\frac{116}{285} \times 71\frac{1}{4} = \frac{1}{2} \times \frac{26336}{285} \times \frac{285}{4} = \frac{1}{2} \times \frac{26336}{1} \times \frac{1}{4} = \frac{26336}{8} = 3292$ cm²
17. % increase $= \frac{\text{(new value} - \text{old value)}}{\text{old value}} \times 100 = \frac{(1192 - 800)}{800} \times 100 = \frac{392}{800} \times 100 = \frac{49}{100} \times 100 = 49\%$
19. Let $x = 0.3888888..$ Therefore, $100x - 10x = 38.888888.. - 3.888888..$
    This simplifies to $90x = 35$, which implies that $x = \frac{35}{90} = \frac{7}{18}$. Denominator = 18
21. Water for Donna $= \frac{2}{5} \times 7000 = 2800$ ml. Water remaining $= 7000 - 2800 = 4200$ ml.
    Water for Anna $= \frac{87}{100} \times 4200 = 3654$ ml. Water for Palin $= 4200 - 3654 = 546$ ml
22. Volume = area of circular cross section × height $= (\pi \times 3^2) \times 8 = 226.19..$ cm³ $= 230$ cm³ to 2 significant figures

Crossword 6 continued

Down

2. Amount made from child subscriptions = £20940 − £16140 = £4800.
   Number of child subscriptions = £4800 ÷ £15 = 320
3. $123 \times 75 = 9225$
4. $208 = 2 \times 2 \times 2 \times 2 \times 13 = 2^4 \times 13$. Therefore, $13 \times 120 = 1560$
5. $\sqrt{1053} + \frac{156}{\sqrt{52}} = \sqrt{81}\sqrt{13} + \frac{156}{\sqrt{4}\sqrt{13}} = 9\sqrt{13} + \frac{156}{\sqrt{4}\sqrt{13}} = 9\sqrt{13} + \frac{78}{\sqrt{13}} = 9\sqrt{13} \times \frac{\sqrt{13}}{\sqrt{13}} + \frac{78}{\sqrt{13}} \times \frac{\sqrt{13}}{\sqrt{13}} = 9\sqrt{13} + \frac{78}{\sqrt{13}} \times \frac{\sqrt{13}}{\sqrt{13}} = 9\sqrt{13} + \frac{78\sqrt{13}}{13} = 9\sqrt{13} + 6\sqrt{13} = 15\sqrt{13}$.
   Therefore, $a = 15$. $a \times 1800 = 15 \times 1800 = 27000$
6. $10 = 2 \times 5$ and $12 = 2 \times 2 \times 3$. HCF = 2. LCM = $2 \times 2 \times 3 \times 5 = 60$. Therefore, both cogs will first return to the same positions in 60 teeth turns. Number of full revolutions of cog A representing 60 teeth turns = $60 \div 10 = 6$.
   Time taken to complete 6 full revolutions = $4.5 \times 6 \times 60 = 1620$ seconds
10. Option 1: biscuits and drink, $5 \times 18 = 90$. Option 2: drink and chewing gum, $18 \times 4 = 72$.
    Option 3: drink, biscuits and chewing gum, $18 \times 5 \times 4 = 360$.
    Total options: $90 + 72 + 360 = 522$
11. $11 \times (27x^9)^{\frac{1}{3}} \div x^{\frac{5}{2}} = \left(11 \times \sqrt[3]{27} \times x^{9 \times \frac{1}{3}}\right) \div x^{\frac{5}{2}} = 33x^3 \div x^{\frac{5}{2}} = 33x^{3-\frac{5}{2}} = 33x^{\frac{1}{2}} = 33\sqrt{4} = 66$
12. $\left(12\frac{2}{5} - 4\frac{4}{25}\right) \times 100 = \left(\frac{62}{5} - \frac{104}{25}\right) \times 100 = \left(\frac{310}{25} - \frac{104}{25}\right) \times 100 = \frac{206}{25} \times 100 = 206 \times 4 = 824$
13. $7^0 \times 7^1 + 5^4 \times 5^{-2} = 7^{0+1} + 5^{4+-2} = 7^1 + 5^2 = 7 + 25 = 32$
15. Radius = $\frac{97}{125} \div 2 = \frac{97}{250} \times \frac{4}{4} = \frac{388}{1000} = 0.388$ m = 388 mm
16. $1125 - (1125 \times 0.16) = 1125 - 180 = 945$
18. $(1.67 + 41.1 + (7.32)^2) \times \sqrt[3]{1015} \approx (2 + 40 + (7)^2) \times \sqrt[3]{1000} = 91 \times 10 = 910$
20. Perimeter lower bound = $a + a + b + b = 22.65 + 22.65 + 18.35 + 18.35 = 82$ cm

Crossword 7

	1	2		3	4
	1	2		3	7
5		6		7	
2		4	6	5		3
8	9			10	
4	2	0		7	1	5
			11		
	8		2	2		0
12		13			14	
1	9	6	0		4	
				15		16
0		5		3	0	3
		17				
1		1	8	6		0

Across

1. $8p + 2p \times 3p - p + 5p = 8p + 6p^2 + 4p = 6p^2 + 12p = 6p(p + 2)$. $a = 6$ and $b = 2$. $a \times b = 6 \times 2 = 12$
3. $(-3x)^2 + (12x - (-2x)) \times 2x = (-3)^2 x^2 + (12x + 2x) \times 2x = 9x^2 + 28x^2 = 37x^2$. Coefficient of x^2 is 37
6. Volume $= (2x + 3)(x + 2)(x - 1) = (2x^2 + 4x + 3x + 6)(x - 1) = x(2x^2 + 7x + 6) - 1(2x^2 + 7x + 6) = 2x^3 + 7x^2 + 6x - 2x^2 - 7x - 6 = 2x^3 + 5x^2 - x - 6$. Coefficient of x^2 term is 5. Therefore, $5 \times 93 = 465$
8. $4(t - 15) + 8(3t + 60) = 4t - 60 + 24t + 480 = 28t + 420$. Value of b is 420
10. $54x^2 - 6 = 6(9x^2 - 1) = 6(3x + 1)(3x - 1)$. Value of b is 3. $718 - b = 718 - 3 = 715$
11. $y^2 + 24y + 44 = (y + 2)(y + 22)$. Value of b is 22
12. $\dfrac{4x + 12}{x^2 + 10x + 21} \div \dfrac{x - 7}{x^3 - 49x} = \dfrac{4(x + 3)}{(x + 3)(x + 7)} \times \dfrac{x(x^2 - 49)}{x - 7} = \dfrac{4}{(x + 7)} \times \dfrac{x(x + 7)(x - 7)}{x - 7} = 4x$. Value of a is 4. Therefore, $a \times 490 = 4 \times 490 = 1960$
15. $y + 2 = 2x + 9$. Therefore, $2x = y + 2 - 9$. $x = \dfrac{y - 7}{2} = \dfrac{613 - 7}{2} = \dfrac{606}{2} = 303$
17. $\dfrac{1}{x} = \dfrac{4}{y^2}$. Therefore, $y^2 = 4x$, $y = \pm\sqrt{4x} = \pm\sqrt{4}\sqrt{x} = \pm 2\sqrt{x} = 2\sqrt{8649} = 2 \times 93 = 186$ as y is positive

Crossword 7 continued

Down

2. $Z = (20^2 - 8(0.25)(20)) \div 6(0.25) = (400 - 40) \div 1.5 = 360 \div 1.5 = 240$
4. $P = 3w\sqrt{v} + 50x = 3(200)(\sqrt{144}) + 50(3) = (600 \times 12) + 150 = 7200 + 150 = 7350$
5. Area $= (5x + 3)(3x + 3) = 15x^2 + 15x + 9x + 9 = 15x^2 + 24x + 9$. Coefficient of x is 24
7. $(m - 22)(m - 26) = m^2 - 26m - 22m + 572 = m^2 - 48m + 572$. Value of b is 572
9. $(2x - 5)^2 + 264 = (2x - 5)(2x - 5) + 264 = 4x^2 - 20x + 25 + 264 = 4x^2 - 20x + 289$. Value of c is 289
11. $3y^2 - 28y - 20 = (3y + 2)(y - 10)$. Value of a is 2. Therefore, $10a = 10 \times 2 = 20$
12. $\frac{6}{x+2} - \frac{3}{(x+2)^2} = \frac{6}{x+2} \times \frac{x+2}{x+2} - \frac{3}{(x+2)^2} = \frac{6(x+2) - 3}{(x+2)^2} = \frac{6x + 12 - 3}{(x+2)^2} = \frac{6x + 9}{(x+2)^2} = \frac{3(2x+3)}{(x+2)^2}$.
    Value of c is 3. Therefore, $98 + c = 98 + 3 = 101$
13. $\frac{1}{x} + \frac{20}{x+5} = \frac{1}{x} \times \frac{x+5}{x+5} + \frac{20}{x+5} \times \frac{x}{x} = \frac{1(x+5) + 20x}{x(x+5)} = \frac{x + 5 + 20x}{x(x+5)} = \frac{21x + 5}{x(x+5)}$. Value of a is 21.
    Therefore, $a \times 31 = 21 \times 31 = 651$
14. $x = \frac{t}{2} - 3x$. Multiply throughout by 2. Therefore, $2x = t - 6x$. $t = 8x$. $t = 8(5) = 40$
15. $\sqrt{2x(y-1)} = 15 - y$. Square both sides. $2x(y-1) = (15-y)^2$. Therefore, $x = \frac{(15-y)^2}{2(y-1)}$.
    $x = \frac{(15-y)^2}{2(y-1)} = \frac{(15-3)^2}{2(3-1)} = \frac{12^2}{2 \times 2} = \frac{144}{4} = 36$
16. $m - 2 = \frac{m - 16}{n}$. Multiply throughout by n. Therefore, $n(m - 2) = m - 16$.
    $mn - 2n = m - 16$. Therefore, $m - mn = 16 - 2n \Rightarrow m(1 - n) = 16 - 2n$.
    Therefore, $m = \frac{16 - 2n}{1 - n} = \frac{16 - 2(0.5)}{1 - 0.5} = \frac{15}{0.5} = 30$

Crossword 8

¹3	2	²6		³1	⁴2	2
9		⁵4	⁶1		6	
⁷1	⁸1		⁹2	1	7	
	¹⁰8	9	9		¹¹5	¹²3
¹³3	0		¹⁴6	¹⁵8		6
1		¹⁶1		¹⁷1	1	0
¹⁸9	8	0		2		1

Across

1. $2x - 400 = 252$. Add 400 to both sides. $2x = 252 + 400$. $2x = 652 \Rightarrow x = 652 \div 2 = 326$
3. $3x - 2x = 65 + 57$. Therefore, $x = 122$
5. $5^{y-38} = 5^3$. Therefore, $y - 38 = 3$. Add 38 to both sides. $y = 3 + 38 = 41$
7. $2^{z-7} = 2^4$. Therefore, $z - 7 = 4$. Add 7 to both sides. $z = 4 + 7 = 11$
9. Let a, b and k be the number of stickers that Alpa, Billy and Kimberly have.
   $b = 2a$, $a = k - 124$ and $a + b + k = 992$.
   Therefore, $a + 2a + (a + 124) = 4a + 124 = 992 \Rightarrow 4a = 868 \Rightarrow a = 868 \div 4 = 217$
10. $x - 500 < 400$. Therefore, $x < 400 + 500 \Rightarrow x < 900$. The largest integer satisfying this is 899
11. Opposite angles are equal in a rhombus. Therefore, $3x - 32 = 2x + 21 \Rightarrow 3x - 2x = 21 + 32$.
    Therefore, $x = 53$ and angle size $= 2x + 21 = 2(53) + 21 = 106 + 21 = 127°$.
    $y = \frac{360° - (2 \times 127°)}{2} = \frac{360° - 254°}{2} = \frac{106°}{2} = 53°$
13. Inequality shown on number line is $x \geq 30$. Smallest integer satisfying this is 30
14. $7x - 150 > 119 + 3x \Rightarrow 7x - 3x > 119 + 150 \Rightarrow 4x > 269 \Rightarrow x > 269 \div 4 \Rightarrow x > 67.25$.
    Smallest integer satisfying this is 68
17. $5x + 1 < 552 \Rightarrow 5x < 552 - 1 \Rightarrow 5x < 551 \Rightarrow x < 110.2$. Largest integer satisfying this is 110
18. Equation 1: $5x - 3y = -47$ and equation 2: $2x + 7y = 383$. Solving by the substitution method, $2x = 383 - 7y \Rightarrow x = 191.5 - 3.5y$ from equation 2. Substituting into equation 1 gives: $5(191.5 - 3.5y) - 3y = -47 \Rightarrow 957.5 - 17.5y - 3y = -47 \Rightarrow 20.5y = 1004.5 \Rightarrow y = 49$ and $x = 191.5 - 3.5y = 191.5 - 3.5(49) = 191.5 - 171.5 = 20$.
    Product of x and y is $xy = 20 \times 49 = 980$

Crossword 8 continued

Down

1. $2x = 798 - 16$. Therefore, $2x = 782 \Rightarrow x = 782 \div 2 = 391$
2. $4x - 100 = 156$. Therefore, $4x = 156 + 100 \Rightarrow x = 256 \div 4 = 64$
4. $x - 1125 = 1550$. Therefore, $x = 1550 + 1125 = 2675$
6. Perimeter of kite $= 2(4x - 0.6) + 2(2.5x) = 8x - 1.2 + 5x = 13x - 1.2$.
   Perimeter of square $= 4(3x) = 12x$. As the perimeters are equal, $13x - 1.2 = 12x \Rightarrow x = 1.2$.
   Square side length $= 3x = 3(1.2) = 3.6$ cm $= 36$ mm. Area of square $= 36 \times 36 = 1296$ mm²
8. Reversing operations from the Output $\Rightarrow$ the Input $= (300 - 30) \div 1.5 = 270 \div 1.5 = 180$
12. $7200 \leq 4n < 7207 \Rightarrow 7200 \div 4 \leq n < 7207 \div 4 \Rightarrow 1800 \leq n < 1801.75$. Therefore, the possible values of n are 1800 and 1801. $1800 + 1801 = 3601$
13. Equation 1: $2x - 6y = 428$ and equation 2: $x + 2y = 389$. Solving by the elimination method, multiply equation 2 by 2 to get equation 3: $2x + 4y = 778$. Subtract equation 1 from equation 3 to leave: $10y = 350 \Rightarrow y = 35$. Substitute $y = 35$ into equation 2 to determine x. Therefore, $x + 2(35) = 389 \Rightarrow x + 70 = 389 \Rightarrow x = 389 - 70 = 319$
15. Equation 1: $-3x + 8y = -62$ and equation 2: $2x - 9y = -10$. Solving by the elimination method, multiply equation 1 by 2 to get equation 3: $-6x + 16y = -124$ and multiply equation 2 by -3 to get equation 4: $-6x + 27y = 30$. Subtract equation 3 from equation 4 to leave: $11y = 154 \Rightarrow y = 14$. Substitute $y = 14$ into equation 2 to determine x. Therefore, $2x - 9(14) = -10 \Rightarrow 2x - 126 = -10 \Rightarrow 2x = -10 + 126 \Rightarrow 2x = 116 \Rightarrow x = 58$. Product of x and y is $xy = 58 \times 14 = 812$
16. Equation 1: $4x + y = 30$ and equation 2: $y = 2x$. Solving by the substitution method, substituting $y = 2x$ into equation 1 gives: $4x + 2x = 30 \Rightarrow 6x = 30 \Rightarrow x = 5$. $y = 2x = 2(5) = 10$

Crossword 9

¹1	5	■	²1	5	³2	■
4	■	⁴4	0	■	7	■
⁵2	⁶3	0	■	⁷2	0	⁸5
■	8	■	⁹3	2	■	0
¹⁰1	7	6	9	■	¹¹1	■
2	■	¹²1	¹³1	5	¹⁴2
¹⁵3	0	0	■	8	■	7

Across

1. The equation of a straight line takes the form of $y = mx + c$ where m is the gradient and c is the y-intercept value. Therefore, for $y = 15x + 11$, $m = 15$
2. The graph with 152 written underneath it is the correct sketch of $y = 2x - 1$ as the y-intercept is -1 and the gradient is positive, $+2$
4. Equation has the form $y = mx + c = -7x + c$. Substitute in $(5, 5)$, $5 = -7(5) + c \Rightarrow c = 5 + 35 = 40$. Equation of the line $y = -7x + 40$. Therefore, $c = 40$
5. Gradient $m = \frac{\text{change in } y}{\text{change in } x} = \frac{5 - -7}{-2 - 6} = \frac{12}{-8} = -\frac{3}{2}$. Equation of line: $y = -\frac{3}{2}x + c$, which goes through $(-2, 5)$. Therefore, $c = y + \frac{3}{2}x = 5 + \frac{3}{2}(-2) = 5 - 3 = 2$. Equation of line: $y = -\frac{3}{2}x + 2$. When $x = -152$, $k = -\frac{3}{2}(-152) + 2 = 228 + 2 = 230$
7. Parallel straight lines have the same gradient. Therefore, the equation of the line will be $y = 15x + c$ and it passes through $(3, 250)$. $c = y - 15x = 250 - 15(3) = 250 - 45 = 205$
9. Parallel straight lines have the same gradient. Therefore, the line AB will have a gradient of 32
10. Midpoint given by $\left(\frac{x_1 + x_2}{2}, \frac{y_1 + y_2}{2}\right) = \left(\frac{38 + 3500}{2}, \frac{1500 + 50}{2}\right) = (1769, 775)$. x-coordinate is 1769
12. $m_{\text{Line 2}} = -\frac{1}{m_{\text{Line 1}}} = -\frac{1}{1/8} = -8$. Therefore, the equation of the line is $y = -8x + c$ and as it passes through $(160, -128)$, $c = y + 8x = -128 + 8(160) = 1280 - 128 = 1152$
15. Shaded area $= \frac{1}{2} \times 30 \times 20 = 300$ units²

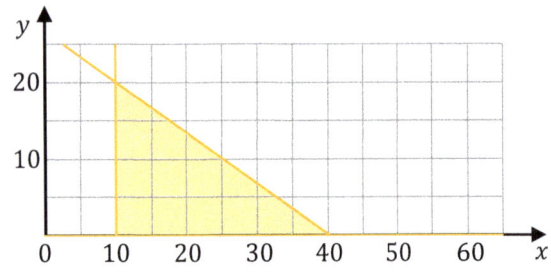

Crossword 9 continued

Down

1. For $y = 103x + 142$, $c = 142$
2. $2y - 20x = 22 \Rightarrow 2y = 20x + 22 \Rightarrow y = 10x + 11$. Gradient is 10
3. $k = 0.5(552) - 6 = 276 - 6 = 270$
4. The straight line $y = 5 + 0.25x$ cuts the y-axis at $(0, 5)$. When $x = 60$, $y = 5 + 0.25(60) = 20$. Therefore, the line goes through points $(0, 5)$ and $(60, 20)$. The graph is shown below. Using the graph, when $y = 15$, $k = 40$

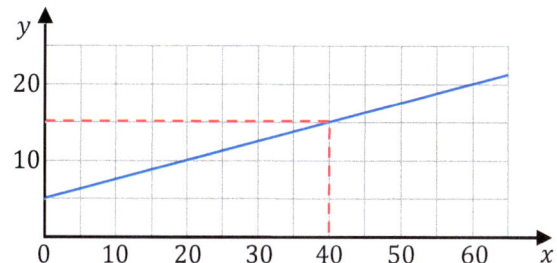

6. Gradient $m = \dfrac{\text{change in } y}{\text{change in } x} = \dfrac{417 - 0}{10 - -129} = \dfrac{417}{139} = 3$. Equation of line: $y = 3x + c$, which goes through $(-129, 0)$. Therefore, $c = y - 3x = 0 - 3(-129) = 387$
7. Equation has the form $y = mx - 31$. Substitute in $(-1, -53)$, $-53 = m(-1) - 31 \Rightarrow m = 53 - 31 = 22$. Equation of the line $y = 22x - 31$. Therefore, $m = 22$
8. For perpendicular lines the product of their gradients is -1. $m_{AB} = -\dfrac{1}{m_{CD}} = -\dfrac{1}{-0.02} = 50$
9. The line crosses the x-axis when $y = 0$. Therefore, $0 = 2x - 782 \Rightarrow 2x = 782 \Rightarrow x = 391$
10. $m = \dfrac{\text{change in } y}{\text{change in } x} = \dfrac{k - 3}{5 - 1} = \dfrac{k - 3}{4} = 30 \Rightarrow k - 3 = 120 \Rightarrow k = 123$
11. $6(y - 3x) = 90 \Rightarrow y - 3x = 15 \Rightarrow y = 3x + 15$. Therefore, $c = 15$
13. Midpoint given by $\left(\dfrac{x_1 + x_2}{2}, \dfrac{y_1 + y_2}{2}\right) = \left(\dfrac{6 + 32}{2}, \dfrac{9 + 27}{2}\right) = (19, 18)$. y-coordinate is 18
14. Equation of line OG is $y = 3x$. Using Pythagoras' Theorem, $x^2 + y^2 = \left(\sqrt{810}\right)^2$. As $y = 3x$, this can be written as $x^2 + (3x)^2 = 810 \Rightarrow x^2 + 9x^2 = 810 \Rightarrow 10x^2 = 810 \Rightarrow x^2 = 81 \Rightarrow x = 9$. $y = 3x = 3(9) = 27$

Crossword 10

¹1	1	■	²1	3	³1	■
⁴4	■	⁴2	8	■	⁵4	5
⁶1	⁷2	■	⁸6	⁹4	0	■
■	¹⁰6	5	■	7	■	■
¹¹2	4	■	■	¹²8	1	¹³9
2	■	¹⁴1	8	0	■	0
¹⁵5	6	5	■	¹⁶1	0	

Across

1. $x^2 - 13x + 22 = 0 \Rightarrow (x-2)(x-11) = 0$. Therefore, $x = 2$ or $x = 11$. Largest solution is 11
2. $\left(x + \frac{6}{2}\right)^2 = (x+3)^2 = x^2 + 6x + 9$. Therefore, $x^2 + 6x + 4 = x^2 + 6x + 9 - 5$.
   Therefore, $(x+3)^2 - 5 = 0 \Rightarrow x + 3 = \pm\sqrt{5} \Rightarrow x = -3 \pm \sqrt{5}$.
   Therefore, $b = 5$ and $b + 126 = 5 + 126 = 131$
4. $x = \frac{-b \pm \sqrt{b^2 - 4ac}}{2a} = \frac{-(-28) \pm \sqrt{(-28)^2 - 4(1)(3)}}{2(1)} = \frac{28 \pm \sqrt{772}}{2}$. Largest solution = 27.89.. = 28
5. $x = \frac{-b \pm \sqrt{b^2 - 4ac}}{2a} = \frac{-90 \pm \sqrt{(90)^2 - 4(-2)(45)}}{2(-2)} = \frac{-90 \pm \sqrt{8460}}{-4}$. Largest solution = 45.49.. = 45
6. The two solutions are $x = 4$ and $x = 12$ when $y = 0$. Largest solution = 12
8. Smallest solution = 4. Therefore, $160 \times 4 = 640$
10. The equation of the quadratic is $y = (x-4)(x-12) = x^2 - 16x + 48$.
    When $x = -1$, $k = (-1)^2 - 16(-1) + 48 = 1 + 16 + 48 = 65$
11. Turning point (minimum) at coordinates $(8, -16)$. Therefore, $8 \times 3 = 24$
12. $x^2 > 4(x+8) \Rightarrow x^2 - 4x - 32 > 0 \Rightarrow (x+4)(x-8) > 0$. This is satisfied by $x < -4$ or $x > 8$.
    Smallest positive integer satisfying this is $x = 9$. Therefore, $91 \times 9 = 819$
14. $x^2 - 12x + 27 \leq 0 \Rightarrow (x-3)(x-9) \leq 0$. This is satisfied by $3 \leq x \leq 9$. Largest positive
    integer satisfying this is $x = 9$. Therefore, $20 \times 9 = 180$
15. From equation 1: $y = 2 - 4x$. Substitute into equation 2: $2 - 4x - x^2 = 5 \Rightarrow x^2 + 4x + 3 = 0$.
    $(x+1)(x+3) = 0$. Therefore, $x = -3$ or $x = -1$. When $x = -3$, $y = 2 - 4(-3) = 14$.
    When $x = -1$, $y = 2 - 4(-1) = 6$. Largest solution for y is $y = 14$. Therefore, $14 + 551 = 565$
16. From equation 2: $y = 10 - x$.
    Substitute into equation 1: $(10-x)^2 + x^2 = 100 \Rightarrow 2x^2 - 20x = 0 \Rightarrow 2x(x-10) = 0$.
    Therefore, $x = 0$ or $x = 10$. When $x = 0$, $y = 10 - 0 = 10$. When $x = 10$, $y = 10 - 10 = 0$.
    Largest solution for y is 10

Crossword 10 continued

Down

1. After expanding, $4x^2 - 13x - 6 = 3x^2 - 12x \Rightarrow x^2 - x - 6 = 0$.
   $x^2 - x - 6 = 0 \Rightarrow (x+2)(x-3) = 0$. Therefore, $x = -2$ or $x = 3$. Therefore, $3 \times 47 = 141$

2. $2\left(x - \frac{4}{2}\right)^2 = 2(x-2)^2 = 2x^2 - 8x + 8$. Therefore, $2x^2 - 8x + 9 = 2x^2 - 8x + 8 + 1$.
   Therefore, $2x^2 - 8x + 9 = 0 \Rightarrow 2(x-2)^2 + 1 = 0$.
   Therefore, $c = 1$ and $187 - c = 187 - 1 = 186$

3. Area of rectangle $= x(x+3) = x^2 + 3x$. Area of triangle $= \frac{1}{2}(4)(3x+2) = 6x + 4$. Area of rectangle = area of triangle. $x^2 + 3x = 6x + 4 \Rightarrow x^2 - 3x - 4 = 0 \Rightarrow (x+1)(x-4) = 0$.
   Therefore, $x = -1$ or $x = 4$. However, $x = 4$ is the only possible answer as one of the sides of the rectangle is x, which cannot be negative. QR $= 3x + 2 = 3(4) + 2 = 14$ cm $= 140$ mm

7. $-1\left(x - \frac{20}{2}\right)^2 = -1(x-10)^2 = -x^2 + 20x - 100$.
   Therefore, $-x^2 + 20x + 164 = -x^2 + 20x - 100 + 264$.
   Therefore, $-x^2 + 20x + 164 = -1(x-10)^2 + 264$. Turning point occurs when $x = 10$, therefore, $-1(10-10)^2 + 264 = 264$

9. $3\left(x + \frac{6}{2}\right)^2 = 3(x+3)^2 = 3(x^2 + 6x + 9) = 3x^2 + 18x + 27$.
   Therefore, $3x^2 + 18x + 15 = 3x^2 + 18x + 27 - 12 = 3(x+3)^2 - 12$. Turning point occurs when $x = -3$, therefore, $3(-3+3)^2 - 12 = -12$. Therefore, $-12 + 4792 = 4780$

11. The x-coordinate of the turning point occurs at $x = -\frac{b}{2a} = -\frac{16}{2(2)} = -4$. At this point, $y = 2(-4)^2 + 16(-4) + 17 = -15$. Therefore, $y^2 = (-15)^2 = 225$

13. $x^2 + 8x - 33 < 0 \Rightarrow (x+11)(x-3) < 0$. This is satisfied by $-11 < x < 3$. Largest positive integer satisfying this is $x = 2$. Therefore, $450 \times 2 = 900$

14. $2x^2 - 3x < x^2 + 28 \Rightarrow x^2 - 3x - 28 < 0 \Rightarrow (x+4)(x-7) < 0$.
    This is satisfied by $-4 < x < 7$. Sum of integer solutions $= -3 + (-2) + (-1) + 0 + 1 + 2 + 3 + 4 + 5 + 6 = 15$

Crossword 11

	1		2		3	
	1	2	3		2	0
4			5			
1	0		6	1	1	
	6	7			8	9
	5	8	2		8	7
			10			
		4	1			2
11				12		
5	4	0		5	2	5
		13				
9		2	1	6		0
14				15		
4	5			3	3	

Across

1. $f(12) = 10(12) + 3 = 120 + 3 = 123$
3. $g(x) = \frac{1}{4}x + 2$. Let $g(x) = x$ and $x = g^{-1}(x)$. Therefore, $4x = g^{-1}(x) + 8 \Rightarrow g^{-1}(x) = 4x - 8$. Therefore, $g^{-1}(7) = 4(7) - 8 = 28 - 8 = 20$
4. $gf(x) = 3(3 - \sqrt{x})^2 + 7 = 3(9 - 6\sqrt{x} + \sqrt{x}\sqrt{x}) + 7 = 27 - 18\sqrt{x} + 3x + 7 = 34 - 18\sqrt{x} + 3x$. $gf(4) = 34 - 18\sqrt{4} + 3(4) = 34 - 36 + 12 = 10$
5. $gf(x) = 7 + 2\left(\frac{x^2+6}{3}\right)$. Therefore, $gf(-30) = 7 + 2\left(\frac{(-30)^2+6}{3}\right) = 7 + 2(302) = 611$
6. $k(8) + 2 = 18 \Rightarrow 8k = 16 \Rightarrow k = 2$. Hence, $g(x) = 2(x - 1) \Rightarrow g(292) = 2(292 - 1) = 582$
8. $x = f^{-1}(x) + 2 \Rightarrow f^{-1}(x) = x - 2$. As $f^{-1}(p) = 85, p - 2 = 85 \Rightarrow p = 85 + 2 = 87$
11. $f(x) = \sin x°$. The graph of $-f(x) = -\sin x°$ is a reflection of $f(x)$ in the x-axis. $-f(x) = -1$ when $x = 90°$ and $x = 450°$. Therefore, $90° + 450° = 540°$
12. $f(x) = x^2 - 3x - 4$ intersects the y-axis when $x = 0 \Rightarrow f(0) = 0^2 - 3(0) - 4 = -4$. The graph of $y = f(x) + 529$ is $f(x)$ moved 529 units up the y-axis. Therefore, $y = f(x) + 529$ will intersect the y-axis when $y = -4 + 529 = 525$
13. As $f(x) = x^3$, the graph of $f(-x)$ is a reflection in the y-axis. Therefore, $f(-x) = (-x)^3 = -x^3$. When $x = -6, y = -(-6)^3 = --216 = 216$
14. For the graph of $f(2x) = \cos 2x°$, the y-coordinate values remain the same but the x-coordinate values are multiplied by $\frac{1}{2}$. Therefore, as $\cos x° = 0$ when $x = 90°$, the x-coordinate values will be half this for $\cos 2x°$. i.e. $x = 45°$
15. Gradient (m_1) of radius $OP = -\frac{5}{2}$. Gradient of tangent $(m_2) = -\frac{1}{m_1} = -\frac{1}{-5/2} = \frac{2}{5}$. Equation of tangent: $y = m_2 x + c = \frac{2}{5}x + c$. Substitute in $(-2, 5) \Rightarrow 5 = \frac{2}{5}(-2) + c \Rightarrow c = \frac{29}{5}$. Equation of tangent: $y = \frac{2}{5}x + \frac{29}{5}$. When $x = 68, y = \frac{2}{5}(68) + \frac{29}{5} = 33$

Crossword 11 continued

Down

1. $f(x) = 3(5 - 2x) = 15 - 6x$.
   Therefore, $ff(x) = 15 - 6(15 - 6x) = 15 - 90 + 36x = 36x - 75$. $ff(5) = 36(5) - 75 = 105$
2. $x = 6g^{-1}(x) + 1 \Rightarrow g^{-1}(x) = \frac{x-1}{6}$. Therefore, $g^{-1}(7) + g(60) = \frac{7-1}{6} + 6(60) + 1 = 362$
3. $fg(x) = 2 + q + qx + p = 223 + 3x$. By equating coefficients, $q = 3$ and $2 + q + p = 223$.
   Therefore, $p = 223 - 2 - q = 223 - 2 - 3 = 218$
7. The graph with 8402 written underneath it is the correct sketch of $y = \frac{1}{x}$
9. The graph with 7250 written underneath it is the correct sketch of $y = 2^{-x}$
10. The roots of $f(x) = -x^3 + 4x$ occur when $-x^3 + 4x = 0 \Rightarrow x(-x^2 + 4) = 0$.
    Therefore, $x = -2, 0, 2$. The graph of $f(x - 521)$ is $f(x)$ moved 521 units right along the x-axis.
    Therefore, it will have roots at $x = -2 + 521, 0 + 521, 2 + 521 = 519, 521, 523$.
    $519 + 521 + 523 = 1563$
11. Point $P(10, k) \Rightarrow 10^2 + k^2 = 101 \Rightarrow k^2 = 101 - 100 \Rightarrow k = 1$. Therefore, $P(10, 1)$.
    Gradient (m_1) of radius $OP = \frac{1}{10}$. Gradient of tangent $(m_2) = -\frac{1}{m_1} = -\frac{1}{1/10} = -10$.
    Equation of tangent: $y = -10x + c$. Substitute in $(10, 1) \Rightarrow 1 = -10(10) + c \Rightarrow c = 101$.
    Equation of tangent: $y = -10x + 101$. When $x = -49.3$, $y = -10(-49.3) + 101 = 594$

Crossword 12

1		2	3		4	
1		2	7		4	7
5	6		7			
6	5		3	6	8	
	8				9	10
	1	4	4		8	6
11			12	13		
1	5		4	8		7
		14		15		
1		1		3	2	
		16				17
5		1	2	0		1
18				19		
6	8	0		2	6	0

Across

2. $x_1 = \sqrt[3]{24 - 2(2)} = 2.71441761659$, $x_2 = 2.64817316916$, $x_3 = 2.7$ to 1 decimal place. Therefore, $2.7 \times 10 = 27$
4. $x_1 = \sqrt{16(15) - 5} = \sqrt{235} = \sqrt{47}\sqrt{5}$. Therefore, $a = 47$
5. $x_1 = \sqrt{7(6) - 3} = 6.24..$, $x_2 = 6.38..$, $x_3 = 6.45..$, $x_4 = 6.49.. = 6.5$ to 2 significant figures. Therefore, $6.5 \times 10 = 65$
7. $U_{n+1} = 2U_n$. Therefore, the 5th term is $U_5 = 2U_4 = 2(184) = 368$
8. This is a sequence of square numbers in descending order. i.e. $16^2, 15^2, 14^2, 13^2, 12^2 = 144$
9. The first seven terms are $p, q, p + q, p + 2q, 2p + 3q, 3p + 5q, 5p + 8q$. The 4th term is 20 and the 6th term is 53. Therefore, $p + 2q = 20$ and $3p + 5q = 53$. $3(20 - 2q) + 5q = 53 \Rightarrow q = 7$. $p + 2(7) = 20 \Rightarrow p = 6$. 7th term $= 5p + 8q = 5(6) + 8(7) = 86$
11. $U_2 = \frac{(2)^2 + 2}{2} = 3$, $U_3 = \frac{(3)^2 + 3}{2} = 6$, $U_4 = \frac{(6)^2 + 6}{2} = 21$. Therefore, $U_4 - U_3 = 21 - 6 = 15$
12. Quadratic sequences take the form of $U_n = an^2 + bn + c$. Substitute in $n = 1, 2$ and 3 to form three equations. Eq 1: $a + b + c = -27$. Eq 2: $4a + 2b + c = -20$. Eq 3: $9a + 3b + c = -9$. Eq 4 = eq 2 − eq 1: $3a + b = 7$. Eq 5 = eq 3 − eq 2: $5a + b = 11$. Eq 5 − Eq 4: $2a = 4 \Rightarrow a = 2$. $3(2) + b = 7 \Rightarrow b = 1$ and $2 + 1 + c = -27 \Rightarrow c = -30$. Therefore, $U_n = 2n^2 + n - 30$ and $U_6 = 2(6)^2 + 6 - 30 = 48$
15. The nth term is given by $U_n = (\sqrt{2})^n$. Therefore, $U_{10} = (\sqrt{2})^{10} = (2^{\frac{1}{2}})^{10} = 2^{\frac{1}{2} \times 10} = 2^5 = 32$
16. The car is stationary on a distance-time graph where the line is horizontal. The car was stationary in the interval between 40 and 80 seconds and in the interval between 100 and 180 seconds, which is a duration of $40 + 80 = 120$ seconds
18. Speed during first 40 seconds = gradient = $\frac{800 - 0}{40 - 0} = 20$ m/s. $700 - 20 = 680$ m/s
19. The train travelled at a constant speed for 35 seconds in the interval between 10 and 45 seconds. $295 - 35 = 260$ seconds

Crossword 12 continued

Down

1. $x_1 = \frac{1}{2} - \frac{(0)^3}{2} = \frac{1}{2}$. $x_2 = \frac{1}{2} - \frac{\left(\frac{1}{2}\right)^3}{2} = \frac{1}{2} - \frac{\frac{1}{8}}{2} = \frac{1}{2} - \frac{1}{16} = \frac{7}{16}$. Denominator = 16
3. $x_1 = 1.2(5100) = 6120$, $x_2 = 1.2(6120) = 7344$
4. $x_1 = \frac{1}{2} - \frac{(0.5)^3}{10} = 0.4875$, $x_2 = 0.4884..$ Therefore, $x = 0.488$ to 3 decimal places. $0.488 \times 1000 = 488$
6. Common difference is 3. The nth term is given by $U_n = 3n + 5$. 170th term = $3(170) + 5 = 515$
10. Common difference is 7. The nth term is given by $U_n = 7n - 3$. 10th term = $7(10) - 3 = 67$
11. Third term = $4^3 + 4^{3-2} = 68$. Fifth term = $4^5 + 4^{5-2} = 1088$. Therefore, $68 + 1088 = 1156$
13. The total distance travelled on a speed-time graph is determined by calculating the area under the graph. Total distance = area of trapezium = $\frac{a+b}{2}h = \frac{(45-10)+(60-0)}{2}(40) = 1900$ metres. Therefore, 10202 metres − 1900 metres = 8302 metres
14. The acceleration on a speed-time graph is determined by calculating the gradient. Acceleration during first 10 seconds = gradient = $\frac{40-0}{10-0} = 4$ m/s². $114 - 4 = 110$ m/s²
17. The train was accelerating for the first 10 seconds

Crossword 13

	1		2	3		4		5
	1		1	1	8	2	1	9
6	5	1	0		6	7		3
	0		6	7	5	2	8	3
		8 1		9 2	0		10 1	1
11 8	0	0	0		12 3	4	2	
		0		13 4	7	9		14 1
15 1	0	16 5	0			9	17 1	8
7		5			18 6	19 4		6
		20 4	5	0		21 5	9	9

Across

2. $5(2y + 6) - 8(5y - 11) = 10y + 30 - 40y + 88 = -30y + 118$. Therefore, $b = 118$
4. $100x^2 - 4 = 4(25x^2 - 1) = 4(5x + 1)(5x - 1)$. Value of b is 5. $224 - b = 224 - 5 = 219$
6. $y(1 + x) = x - 1021 \Rightarrow y + xy = x - 1021 \Rightarrow x - xy = y + 1021 \Rightarrow x = \frac{y + 1021}{1 - y} = \frac{-1 + 1021}{1 - (-1)} = 510$
7. Perimeters are equal: $2(1.2x) + 2(3x - 4) = 2(x + 1) + 2(11)$.
   Therefore, $2.4x + 6x - 8 = 2x + 2 + 22 \Rightarrow 6.4x = 32 \Rightarrow x = 5$.
   Area of 8 identical rectangles $= 8 \times 11 \times (5 + 1) = 528$ cm²
9. Gradient $(m) = \frac{4 - -2}{3 - -3} = \frac{6}{6} = 1$. Equation of line $y = mx + c \Rightarrow y = x + c \Rightarrow c = y - x$.
   Substitute in $(3, 4) \Rightarrow c = 4 - 3 = 1$. Therefore, $y = x + 1$. When $x = 19$, $k = 19 + 1 = 20$
10. Midpoint given by $\left(\frac{x_1 + x_2}{2}, \frac{y_1 + y_2}{2}\right) = \left(\frac{-5 + 27}{2}, \frac{2 + 8}{2}\right) = (11, 5)$. x-coordinate is 11
11. Area of trapezium $= \frac{1}{2}(a + b)h = \frac{1}{2}(2x + 1 + 5x - 3)(2x) = 7x^2 - 2x$. Area of square $= x^2$.
    Area of trapezium $= 6 \times$ area of square. $7x^2 - 2x = 6x^2 \Rightarrow x^2 - 2x = 0 \Rightarrow x(x - 2) = 0$.
    Therefore, $x = 0$ or $x = 2$. As x cannot equal 0, the side length of the square is 2 m and its perimeter is 8 m $= 8000$ mm
12. $x = \frac{-b \pm \sqrt{b^2 - 4ac}}{2a} = \frac{-(-9) \pm \sqrt{(-9)^2 - 4(1)(4)}}{2(1)} = \frac{9 \pm \sqrt{65}}{2}$. Largest solution $= 8.53.. = 9$. $351 - 9 = 342$
13. From equation 2: $y = 3 - x^2$. Substitute this into equation 1: $3 - x^2 + 5x = -3$.
    Therefore, $x^2 - 5x - 6 = 0 \Rightarrow (x + 1)(x - 6) = 0$. When $x = -1$, $y = 3 - (-1)^2 = 2$.
    When $x = 6$, $y = 3 - (6)^2 = -33$. Largest solution is $x = 6$. Therefore, $6 + 473 = 479$
15. $gf(x) = 2(3 + 2x)^2 - 8 = 2(9 + 12x + 4x^2) - 8 = 18 + 24x + 8x^2 - 8 = 8x^2 + 24x + 10$.
    $gf(10) = 8(10)^2 + 24(10) + 10 = 800 + 240 + 10 = 1050$
17. $4 \times 2^{k-14} = 64 \Rightarrow 2^{k-14} = 16 \Rightarrow 2^{k-14} = 2^4 \Rightarrow k - 14 = 4 \Rightarrow k = 4 + 14 = 18$
18. $x_1 = \sqrt[3]{70 + 30(7)} = 6.542..$, $x_2 = 6.433..$, $x_3 = 6.406.. = 6.4$ to 1 decimal place. $6.4 \times 10 = 64$
20. Total distance = area of trapezium $= \frac{a + b}{2}h = \frac{(15 - 5) + (20 - 0)}{2}(30) = 450$ metres
21. $\frac{x + 1}{60} = 10 \Rightarrow x + 1 = 600 \Rightarrow x = 600 - 1 = 599$

Crossword 13 continued

Down

1. Area $= \frac{1}{2}(x+2)(2x-1) = \frac{1}{2}(2x^2+3x-2) = x^2+\frac{3}{2}x-1$. Therefore, $\frac{3}{2}(100) = 150$
2. $2x - 12 = 3x - 118 \Rightarrow 3x - 2x = -12 + 118 \Rightarrow x = 106$
3. $\frac{8}{x} + \frac{4}{x+2} = 5 \Rightarrow \left(\frac{8}{x} \times \frac{x+2}{x+2}\right) + \left(\frac{4}{x+2} \times \frac{x}{x}\right) = 5 \Rightarrow \frac{8x+16+4x}{x^2+2x} = 5 \Rightarrow 12x+16 = 5(x^2+2x)$.
   Therefore, $5x^2 - 2x - 16 = 0 \Rightarrow (x-2)(5x+8) = 0 \Rightarrow x = 2$ or $x = -\frac{8}{5}$.
   Largest solution = 2. Therefore, $2 \times 4325 = 8650$
4. $7x - 119 > 6x + 158 \Rightarrow x > 277$. Smallest integer satisfying this is 278
5. Equation 1: $2x + 11y = 51$ and equation 2: $x - 5y = -6 \Rightarrow x = 5y - 6$. Substitute into equation 1: $2(5y-6) + 11y = 51 \Rightarrow 21y = 63 \Rightarrow y = 3$ and $x = 5(3) - 6 = 9$.
   Therefore, $9340 - x = 9340 - 9 = 9331$
8. Gradient of line A is -4. Equation of A: $y = -4x + c \Rightarrow c = y + 4x$. Substitute in $(200, 200) \Rightarrow c = 200 + 4(200) = 1000$. Therefore, the y-intercept is 1000
9. Gradient of line B is $-\frac{1}{1/5} = -5$. Equation of line B: $y = -5x + c \Rightarrow c = y + 5x$. Substitute in $(300, 540) \Rightarrow c = 540 + 5(300) = 2040$. Therefore, the y-intercept is 2040
10. The graph of $y = \frac{3}{4}x - 2$ passes through the point $(0, -2)$. When $x = 16$, $y = \frac{3}{4}(16) - 2 = 10$.
    Therefore, $y = \frac{3}{4}x - 2$ passes through $(0, -2)$ and $(16, 10)$. The green line on the graph shows a sketch of $y = \frac{3}{4}x - 2$. The solution to the two simultaneous equations is the point where they cross, which is at point $(8, 4)$. Therefore, $8 + 4 = 12$

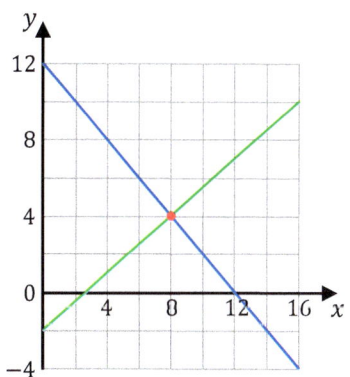

12. $x = \frac{1}{12}g^{-1}(x) - 3 \Rightarrow \frac{1}{12}g^{-1}(x) = x + 3 \Rightarrow g^{-1}(x) = 12(x+3)$.
    Therefore, $g^{-1}(330) = 12(330 + 3) = 3996$
14. $\left(x + \frac{16}{2}\right)^2 = (x+8)^2 = x^2 + 16x + 64$. Therefore, $x^2 + 16x + 21 = x^2 + 16x + 64 - 43$.
    Therefore, $(x+8)^2 - 43 = 0 \Rightarrow x + 8 = \pm\sqrt{43} \Rightarrow x = -8 \pm \sqrt{43}$.
    Therefore, $b = 43$ and $b + 1826 = 43 + 1826 = 1869$
15. $f(x) = -x^2 + 7x + 255$ intersects the y-axis when $x = 0 \Rightarrow f(0) = -(0)^2 + 7(0) + 255 = 255$.
    The graph of $y = f(x) - 78$ is $f(x)$ moved 78 units down the y-axis. Therefore, $y = f(x) - 78$ will intersect the y-axis when $y = 255 - 78 = 177$
16. Common difference is 12. The nth term is given by $U_n = 12n + 2$. 46th term $= 12(46) + 2 = 554$
19. The turning point of $x^2 - 30x + 200$ occurs at $x = -\frac{b}{2a} = -\frac{-30}{2(1)} = 15$ and the value of $y = (15)^2 - 30(15) + 200 = -25$. Therefore, $T(15, -25)$. Straight line passing through $T(15, -25)$ and $O(0, 0)$ is $y = \frac{-25-0}{15-0}x \Rightarrow y = -\frac{5}{3}x$. When $x = -27$, $k = -\frac{5}{3}(-27) = 45$

Crossword 14

1 3	6		2 8	1	3 6	
2		4 1	0		5 1	7
6 2	7 1	6		8 4	0	
	0		9 2	8		10 5
11 3	6	4	5		12 2	0
	0		13 5	7	2	
14 1	0	0			15 4	2

Across

1. 48 red pens are equal to 4 parts. 1 part = $\frac{48}{4}$ = 12 pens. There are $3 \times 12 = 36$ green pens
2. The girls make up 2 more parts of the ratio than boys $(7 - 5)$, which corresponds to 136 students. 1 part = $\frac{136}{2}$ = 68 students. Total number of students = $(5 \times 68) + (7 \times 68) = 816$
4. $\frac{3x-8}{8x+19} = \frac{2}{9}$. Therefore, $9(3x - 8) = 2(8x + 19) \Rightarrow 27x - 16x = 72 + 38 \Rightarrow x = 10$
5. Number of litres of yellow paint required per 10 litre pot of green paint = $\frac{2}{5} \times 10 = 4$ litres.
   Number of litres of blue paint required per 10 litre pot of green paint = $\frac{3}{5} \times 10 = 6$ litres.
   Cost of buying paint to produce 10 litres of green paint = $(£3.85 \times 4) + (£4.10 \times 6) = £40$.
   Profit from sales of each pot = $£57 - £40 = £17$
6. Linear scale factor = 5 : 6. Volume scale factor = $5^3 : 6^3 = 125 : 216$. Answer = 216
8. Linear scale factor = $\sqrt{4} : \sqrt{25} = 2 : 5$. Volume scale factor = $2^3 : 5^3 = 8 : 125$.
   Volume of S1 = $\frac{8}{125} \times 625 = 40$ cm^3
9. The graph with 28 written underneath it shows a sketch of $y \propto x$
11. $a \propto b^3 \Rightarrow a = kb^3$. Therefore, $k = a \div b^3 = 40 \div 2^3 = 5$. Therefore, $a = 5b^3 = 5(9^3) = 3645$
12. $c \propto \frac{1}{d^2} \Rightarrow c = \frac{k}{d^2}$. Therefore, $k = cd^2 = 5(4^2) = 80$. Therefore, $c = \frac{80}{d^2} = \frac{80}{2^2} = \frac{80}{4} = 20$
13. $y = k\sqrt{x} \Rightarrow k = y \div \sqrt{x} = 36 \div \sqrt{81} = 4$. Therefore, $y = 4\sqrt{x} = 4(\sqrt{20449}) = 572$
14. $y = \frac{k}{x}$. Therefore, $k = xy = 10(50) = 500$. Therefore, $y = \frac{500}{x} = \frac{500}{5} = 100$
15. $y = kx^2 \Rightarrow k = y \div x^2 = 0.5 \div 1^2 = 0.5$. Therefore, $y = 0.5x^2 \Rightarrow p = \sqrt{4} = 2$, $q = 0.5(8^2) = 32$ and $r = 0.5(4^2) = 8$. Therefore, $p + q + r = 2 + 32 + 8 = 42$

Crossword 14 continued

Down
1. 92 children are equal to 2 parts. 1 part = $\frac{92}{2}$ = 46 people. Therefore, there are $5 \times 46 = 230$ adults. Total number of people = $230 + 92 = 322$
2. Number of headed goals = $0.2 \times 240 = 48$. Goals scored with feet = $240 - 48 = 192$. There are 3 parts to the ratio with each part representing $\frac{192}{3} = 64$ goals. Number of goals scored with right foot = $1 \times 64 = 64$ and left foot = $2 \times 64 = 128$. Therefore, $128 - 48 = 80$
3. 1 part of the ratio = $\frac{2135}{7} = 305$ grams. Therefore, sugar needed = $2 \times 305 = 610$ grams
4. The ratio of yellow to purple marbles is 4 : 1 and the ratio of purple to blue marbles is 2 : 1. The number of purple marbles links the two ratios. Multiplying the first ratio by 2 gives 8 : 2. The purple marbles part of each ratio is now the same. Therefore, the ratio of yellow to purple to blue marbles is 8 : 2 : 1. There are 2 blue marbles which equals 1 part of the ratio. Therefore, the number of yellow marbles = $8 \times 2 = 16$
7. $0.2 \times 5.3 = 1.06$ m² = $1.06 \times 100 \times 100 = 10600$ cm² as 1 m = 100 cm
8. Longer side on smaller rectangle = x. Therefore, $\frac{4}{10} = \frac{x}{30} \Rightarrow 10x = 120 \Rightarrow x = 12$ cm. Area of smaller rectangle = $12 \times 4 = 48$ cm²
9. Volume scale factor = 64 : 27. Linear scale factor = $\sqrt[3]{64} : \sqrt[3]{27} = 4 : 3$. Height of C2 = $\frac{3}{4} \times 34 = 25.5$ cm = 255 mm
10. $\frac{8}{12} = \frac{x}{7.5} \Rightarrow 12x = 60 \Rightarrow x = 5$ cm = 50 mm
12. Linear scale factor = 12 : 8 = 3 : 2. Volume scale factor = $3^3 : 2^3 = 27 : 8$. Volume of smaller cuboid = $\frac{8}{27} \times 756 = 224$ cm³

Crossword 15

	1	2		3			4
	3	2		9	2		1
		5				6	
		1	2	0		9	9
	7			8			
	6	0		4	8	7	
			9			10	11
			1	0		2	1
12					13		
3	5	3			2		4
			14				
0			2	8	7	4	3
0			6		5		4

Across

1. Gradient = $\frac{\text{change in } y}{\text{change in } x} = \frac{18 - 3.2}{9.2 - 0} = \frac{14.8}{9.2} = 1.60.. = 1.6$ m/s² to 1 decimal place. $1.6 \times 20 = 32$

3. Distance $= \frac{1}{2}(0 + 5.6)(2) + \frac{1}{2}(5.6 + 9.6)(2) + \frac{1}{2}(9.6 + 12)(2) + \frac{1}{2}(12 + 12.8)(2) + \frac{1}{2}(12.8 + 12)(2) = 92$ metres

5. Average acceleration $= \frac{\text{speed}}{\text{time}} = \frac{12 - 0}{10 - 0} = 1.2$ m/s². $1.2 \times 100 = 120$

6. 27.5 m in 1 second = 0.0275 km in 1 second = (0.0275×3600) km in 1 hour = 99 km/h

7. Speed $= \frac{\text{distance}}{\text{time}} \Rightarrow$ distance = speed × time $= 45 \times \frac{80}{60} = 45 \times \frac{4}{3} = 60$ km

8. Pressure $= \frac{\text{force}}{\text{area}} \Rightarrow$ force = pressure × area $= 121750 \times 0.004 = 487$ N

9. Density $= \frac{\text{mass}}{\text{volume}}$. Volume of metal A $= \frac{\text{mass}}{\text{density}} = \frac{120}{8} = 15$. Volume of metal B $= \frac{160}{13} = 12.30..$
   Total volume of alloy = 27.30.. cm³. Total mass of alloy = 280 g.
   Density of alloy $= \frac{280}{27.30..} = 10.25..$
   Therefore, the alloy has a density of 10 g/cm³ to the nearest whole number

10. $(0.8)^4 \times £51 = £20.89 = £21$ to the nearest whole pound

12. Money made at end of year 1: $1.03 \times £5000 = £5150$, year 2: $1.02 \times £5150 = £5253$, year 3: $1.019 \times £5253 = £5352.81$. Profit made $= £5352.81 - £5000 = £352.81 = £353$ to the nearest whole pound

14. Population by end of 2021 (i.e. in 4 years) $= (1.036)^4 \times 24951 = 28742.66.. = 28743$ rounded to the nearest person

Crossword 15 continued

Down

2. Average speed $= \frac{\text{distance}}{\text{time}} = \frac{100 - 0}{10 - 0} = 10$ m/s. $10 \times 21 = 210$
3. Gradient $= \frac{\text{change in } y}{\text{change in } x} = \frac{64 - 0}{10 - 2} = \frac{64}{8} = 8$ m/s. $8 \times 1130 = 9040$
4. 70 km in 1 hour = 70000 m in 1 hour = 70000 m in 60 minutes = 70000 m in 3600 seconds = $\frac{70000}{3600} = 19.\dot{4} = 19$ metres per second to the nearest whole number
6. Speed $= \frac{\text{distance}}{\text{time}} \Rightarrow$ time $= \frac{\text{distance}}{\text{speed}} = \frac{1.512}{5.6} = 0.27$ hours $= 0.27 \times 60 \times 60 = 972$ seconds
9. Area of circle $= \pi \times (0.12)^2 = 0.045..$ m². Pressure $= \frac{\text{force}}{\text{area}} = \frac{60}{0.045..} = 1326.29.. = 1326$ N/m² to the nearest whole number
11. Cube edge length = 0.75 m = 75 cm. Volume of cube $= (75)^3 = 421875$ cm³. Mass = density × volume = $3.4 \times 421875 = 1434375$ g = 1434.375 kg = 1434 kg
12. The profit at the end of each of the three years is identical with simple interest. Profit at end of each year = $(1.02 \times £5000) - £5000 = £100$. Profit at end of 3 years $= 3 \times £100 = £300$
13. Compound interest $= ((1.018)^3 \times £5000) - £5000 = £274.89 = £275$ to the nearest whole pound

Page | 94

Crossword 16

	1		2			3		4
1	1	8	7	5	■	1	4	5
2	2	■	5	6	■	4	■	2
			2	9				
7	8	8	0	9	3	0	■	5
	8	1		6				
	■	9	■	10	■	■	11	
				3	0		7	0
12	1	13	2	■	14	1	4	2	■
		4						
■	■	9	■	15	4	1	■	9	■
16	8	17	7	5	■	■	1	18	6	19	1
20	8	8	8	■	21	3	6	22	2	■	2
	■	23	1	7	2	■	4		5

Across

1. 675 fiction books are equal to 9 parts. 1 part = $\frac{675}{9}$ = 75 books. There are $16 \times 75 = 1200$ non-fiction books. Therefore, there are $675 + 1200 = 1875$ books in total

3. Number of litres of cordial required per 2 litre bottle = $\left(\frac{1}{4} \times 2\right)$ litres = 500 millilitres.
   Number of litres of water required per 2 litre bottle = $\left(\frac{3}{4} \times 2\right)$ litres = 1500 millilitres.
   Cost of buying liquids to produce a 2 litre bottle = $(£1.25 \times 1) + (£0.4 \times 3) = £2.45$.
   Profit from sales of each bottle = $£3.90 - £2.45 = £1.45 = 145$ pence

5. $\frac{3x+2}{x+5} = \frac{x-2}{2x-13}$. Therefore, $(3x+2)(2x-13) = (x+5)(x-2)$.
   $6x^2 - 35x - 26 = x^2 + 3x - 10 \Rightarrow 5x^2 - 38x - 16 = 0 \Rightarrow (5x+2)(x-8) = 0$.
   Therefore, $x = -\frac{2}{5}$ and $x = 8$. Largest solution is 8. Answer = $8 \times 3.625 = 29$

7. Vertical side on larger triangle = x. Therefore, $\frac{4}{36} = \frac{5}{x} \Rightarrow 4x = 180 \Rightarrow x = 45$ cm.
   Area of larger triangle = $\frac{1}{2} \times 36 \times 45 = 810$ cm²

9. Linear scale factor = $\sqrt{461} : \sqrt{165}$. Volume scale factor = $\left(\sqrt{461}\right)^3 : \left(\sqrt{165}\right)^3$.
   Volume of P1 = $\frac{\left(\sqrt{461}\right)^3}{\left(\sqrt{165}\right)^3} \times 135 = 630$ cm³ to the nearest whole number

10. Volume scale factor = $125 : 729$. Linear scale factor = $\sqrt[3]{125} : \sqrt[3]{729} = 5 : 9$.
    Width of C1 = $\frac{5}{9} \times 54 = 30$ cm

11. $y = kx \Rightarrow k = y \div x = 6 \div 3 = 2$. Therefore, $y = 2x = 2(35) = 70$

12. $y = \frac{k}{x}$. Therefore, $k = xy = 9(23) = 207$. Therefore, $y = \frac{207}{x} = \frac{207}{1/6} = 207 \times 6 = 1242$

14. Population by end of 2022 (i.e. in 6 years) = $(0.994)^6 \times 4000 = 3858.14..$
    Therefore, the population fell by $4000 - 3858.14.. = 142$ people rounded to the nearest person

15. Distance = $\frac{1}{2}(0+1)(1) + \frac{1}{2}(1+2.5)(1) + \frac{1}{2}(2.5+5)(1) + \frac{1}{2}(5+8.5)(1) +$
    $\frac{1}{2}(8.5+13.5)(1) + \frac{1}{2}(13.5+20)(1) = 41$ m to the nearest whole metre

Crossword 16 continued

Across continued

17. $y = \frac{k}{x}$. The constant k always remains the same. If $x = 1$ and $y = 1$ then $k = 1$. Given that x decreases by 43%, it becomes $0.57 \times 1 = 0.57$. Therefore, $y = \frac{1}{0.57} = 1.75..$
% increase in $y = \frac{(\text{new value} - \text{old value})}{\text{old value}} \times 100 = \frac{(1.75.. - 1)}{1} \times 100 = 75\%$ to the nearest integer

18. Density $= \frac{\text{mass}}{\text{volume}}$. Volume of metal A $= \frac{\text{mass}}{\text{density}} = \frac{170}{48} = \frac{85}{24}$. Volume of metal B $= \frac{220}{76} = \frac{55}{19}$.
Total volume of alloy $= \frac{85}{24} + \frac{55}{19} = \frac{2935}{456}$ cm³. Total mass of alloy = 390 g.
Density of alloy $= \frac{390}{2935/456} = 61$ g/cm³ to the nearest whole number

20. Compound interest $= ((1.12)^4 \times £1548) - £1548 = £888$ to the nearest pound

21. Pressure $= \frac{\text{force}}{\text{area}} = \frac{18.1}{0.05} = 362$ N/m²

23. The amount at the end of 2 years $= \left(1 + \frac{x}{100}\right)^2 \times £100 = £143.35$.
Therefore, $\frac{x}{100} = \sqrt{1.4335} - 1 \Rightarrow x = 100(\sqrt{1.4335} - 1) = 19.72..\%$.
At the end of three years $= \left(1 + \frac{19.72..}{100}\right)^3 \times £100 = £172$ to the nearest whole pound

Down

1. Isaac had 5 more parts of the ratio than Janya $(7 - 2)$, which corresponds to £160.
1 part $= \frac{160}{5} = £32$. Isaac had 4 more parts of the ratio than Karl $(7 - 3)$, which $= 4 \times £32 = £128$

2. 4 parts of the ratio account for 2D shapes, 70% of which are yellow $= \left(\frac{7}{10} \times 4\right) = \frac{14}{5}$ parts.
3 parts of the ratio account for 3D shapes, 28% of which are yellow $= \left(\frac{28}{100} \times 3\right) = \frac{21}{25}$ parts.
Total number of parts $= 4 + 3 = 7$. Total number of yellow parts $= \frac{14}{5} + \frac{21}{25} = \frac{91}{25}$.
Percentage of parts which are yellow $= \frac{91/25}{7} \times 100 = \frac{13}{25} \times 100 = 52\%$

3. Sum of ratio parts $= 8 + 7 + 5 = 20$. 1 part $= \frac{5000}{20} = 250$ grams. Amount of each ingredient required to make the mixture: sugar $= 8 \times 250 = 2000$ grams $= \frac{2000}{200} = 10$ bags of sugar, syrup $= 7 \times 250 = 1750$ grams $= \frac{1750}{250} = 7$ pots of syrup, butter $= 5 \times 250 = 1250$ grams $= \frac{1250}{250} = 5$ pots of butter. Cost of ingredients $= (10 \times £0.50) + (7 \times £0.80) + (5 \times £1.60) = £18.60$. Number of sweets made $= \frac{5000}{10} = 500$. Revenue from sales $= 500 \times £0.04 = £20$.
Profit made $= £20 - £18.60 = £1.40 = 140$ pence

4. $x + 22 : 3 = 8 : 1$. Therefore, $1(x + 22) = 8 \times 3 \Rightarrow x = 2$. Therefore, the ratio of time taken to complete tasks A and B is $2 : 3$. 2 parts = 3500 minutes, therefore, 1 part = 1750 minutes. 3 parts for task B = $3 \times 1750 = 5250$ minutes

6. $\frac{a}{c} = \frac{b}{d} \Rightarrow \frac{8}{24} = \frac{15}{d} \Rightarrow 8d = 360 \Rightarrow d = 45$ cm. Larger parallelogram area $= 24 \times 45 = 1080$ cm².
Smaller parallelogram area $= 8 \times 15 = 120$ cm². Shaded area $= 1080 - 120 = 960$ cm²

8. $0.32 \times 6 = 1.92$ cm² $= 1.92 \times 10 \times 10 = 192$ mm² as 1 cm = 10 mm

10. The graph with 32 written underneath it shows a sketch of $y \propto \frac{1}{x}$

11. Gradient $= \frac{\text{change in } y}{\text{change in } x} = \frac{16.5 - 0}{6 - 1.9} = \frac{16.5}{4.1} = 4$ m/s² to the nearest whole number. $4 \times 1824 = 7296$

13. Acceleration $= \frac{\text{speed}}{\text{time}} = \frac{20 - 0}{6 - 0} = 3$ m/s² to the nearest whole number. $49778 + 3 = 49781$ m/s²

14. 310 m in 1 second = 0.31 km in 1 second = (0.31×3600) km in 1 hour = 1116 km/h

16. Pressure $= \frac{\text{force}}{\text{area}} = \frac{66}{0.075} = 880$ N/m²

19. Volume $= \frac{\text{mass}}{\text{density}} = \frac{1000}{8} = 125$ cm³

21. Speed $= \frac{\text{distance}}{\text{time}} = \frac{96}{3} = 32$ miles per hour

22. Simple interest $= 3 \times ((1.025 \times £320) - £320) = £24$

Page | 96

Crossword 17

	1	2		3	4
	8	1		6 0	9
5		6			
3		3	3 0		5
7	8			9	
1	1	3		7	2
			10		
	5		4 3 2		
11		12			13
2	7	5 0			6
			14		
3		0	1 1 0		
		15			
9		5 6 0			

Across

1. Interior angles in a pentagon sum to 540°. $x = 540° - (141° + 146° + 68° + 104°) = 81°$
3. Interior angles in a heptagon sum to 900° and interior angles in a decagon sum to 1440°. The interior angle size in a regular heptagon $= \frac{900°}{7} = 128.57..°$ and the interior angle size in a regular decagon $= \frac{1440°}{10} = 144°$.
   As angles at a point sum to 360°, $x = 360° - (128.57..° + 144°) = 87°$ to the nearest whole number. Therefore, $87° \times 7 = 609°$
6. As alternate angles are equal, ∠BFE = ∠IFE = u and as angles around a point sum to 360°, $x = 360° - 2u = 360° - 2(15°) = 330°$
7. Condition SAS means that two sides and the included angle in T5 are equal to two sides and the included angle in T6. Therefore, $b = 113°$
9. Perimeter of rectangle $= 2(2x - 4) + 2(4x - 10.4) = 12x - 28.8 =$ perimeter of hexagon. Side length (S) of hexagon $= \frac{12x - 28.8}{6} = 2x - 4.8$. When $x = 6$, S $= 2(6) - 4.8 = 7.2$ cm $= 72$ mm
10. Perimeter of hexagon $= 6 \times 72 = 432$ mm
11. Area of triangle $= \frac{1}{2} \times b \times h = \frac{1}{2} \times 550 \times 10 = 2750$ mm²
14. Area of rectangle $= (2x - 4)(4x - 10.4) = (2(6) - 4)(4(6) - 10.4) = 108.8$ cm² $= 110$ cm² to 2 significant figures
15. $A = bh \Rightarrow h = \frac{A}{b} = \frac{7}{1.25} = 5.6$ m $= 560$ cm

Crossword 17 continued

Down

2. As corresponding angles are equal, $2x + 11 = 3x - 7 \Rightarrow x = 18$. Hence, $(2(18) + 11)° = 47°$. As angles on a straight line sum to 180°, $y = 180° - 47° = 133°$
3. Exterior angle $= \frac{360°}{n} = \frac{360°}{6} = 60°$
4. ∠ABE and ∠DEB are supplementary angles, which sum to 180°. ∠ABE $= 180° - 124° = 56°$. As ∠ABE = ∠CBF and angles at a point sum to 180°, $x = 180° - (2 \times 56°) = 68°$. Therefore, $68° \times 14 = 952°$
5. Condition SSS means that all three sides in T1 are equal to the three sides in T2. Therefore, the perimeter of T1 will equal the perimeter of T2. Perimeter $= 6.5 + 14.1 + 10.4 = 31$ cm
8. Condition RHS means that both triangles have a right angle, an equal hypotenuse and one other equal side. The hypotenuse is the longest side on a right-angled triangle $= 157$ mm
9. Height of rectangle $x = \frac{A}{w} = \frac{40}{20} = 2$ cm. Area of trapezium $= \frac{1}{2}(a + b)h = \frac{1}{2}(20 + 5x + 6)(2x)$. Substitute in $x = 2 \Rightarrow$ Area of trapezium $= \frac{1}{2}(26 + 5(2))(2(2)) = 72$ cm²
10. Perimeter of square $= 4 \times 10 = 40$ cm
11. Area of triangle $= \frac{1}{2}ab \sin C = \frac{1}{2}(4)(13)(\sin 113°) = 23.93..$ cm². Area of 10 such triangles $= 10 \times 23.93.. = 239$ cm² to the nearest whole number
12. Area of BEF $= \frac{1}{2}ab \sin C = \frac{1}{2}(33)(33)(\sin 68°) = 505$ cm² to the nearest whole number
13. Using Pythagoras' theorem, height of T4 $= \sqrt{(15.7)^2 - (12.3)^2} = 9.75..$ cm. Area of triangle $= \frac{1}{2} \times b \times h = \frac{1}{2} \times 12.3 \times 9.75.. = 60$ cm² to the nearest whole number
14. A decagon has 10 sides

Crossword 18

	1	2			3	
	1	6	8		1	8
4				5		
2		3		4	4	
6	7		8			9
1	1	7	2	5		2
					10	
	0		5		1	8
11			12	13		
4	0		2	8		9
		14		15	16	
8		9		6	4	6
17						
1	2	0	0		2	

Across

1. $\mathbf{a} + \mathbf{b} = \begin{pmatrix} 5+7 \\ 4+10 \end{pmatrix} = \begin{pmatrix} 12 \\ 14 \end{pmatrix}$. Therefore, $m = 12$, $n = 14$ and $mn = 12 \times 14 = 168$
3. $\mathbf{c} = 2\mathbf{a}$. Therefore, $k = 2$ and $k \times 9 = 2 \times 9 = 18$
5. $\overrightarrow{AB} = \overrightarrow{AO} + \overrightarrow{OB} = -21\mathbf{a} + 14\mathbf{b}$ and $\overrightarrow{OC} = \overrightarrow{OA} + \overrightarrow{AC} = \overrightarrow{OA} + \frac{2}{7}\overrightarrow{AB} = 21\mathbf{a} + \frac{2}{7}(-21\mathbf{a} + 14\mathbf{b}) = 15\mathbf{a} + 4\mathbf{b}$. Therefore, $k = 15$, $n = 4$ and $4(k - n) = 4(15 - 4) = 4(11) = 44$
6. $\overrightarrow{AD} = \overrightarrow{AB} + \overrightarrow{BD} = \overrightarrow{AB} + \frac{4}{5}\overrightarrow{BC} = 25\mathbf{b} + \frac{4}{5}(10\mathbf{a}) = 8\mathbf{a} + 25\mathbf{b}$.
   Therefore, $k = 8$, $n = 25$ and $n \times 469 = 25 \times 469 = 11725$
10. After the translation, shape B has corners at coordinates $(-4, 2), (-2, 2), (-2, 4)$ and $(-4, 4)$. The centre of shape B is at coordinates $(-3, 3)$. Therefore, $3 \times 6 = 18$
11. After the reflection, shape C has corners at coordinates $(1, -3), (3, -3), (3, -5)$ and $(1, -5)$. The centre of shape C is at coordinates $(2, -4)$. Therefore, $-4 \times -10 = 40$
12. After the rotation, shape D has corners at coordinates $(3, 3), (3, 5), (5, 5)$ and $(5, 3)$. The centre of shape D is at coordinates $(4, 4)$. Therefore, $4 \times 7 = 28$
15. Invariant points are points that remain in the same position after the transformation has taken place. The only corner which remains the same on shape D is the point of rotation $(3, 3)$. Hence, the number of invariant points is 1. Therefore, $647 - 1 = 646$
17. After the enlargement, shape E has corners at coordinates $(-6, 1), (-2, 1), (-2, -3)$ and $(-6, -3)$. The centre of shape E is at coordinates $(-4, -1)$. Therefore, $-4 \times -300 = 1200$

Page | 99

Crossword 18 continued

Down

2. $\mathbf{a} - \mathbf{b} = \begin{pmatrix} 2 - (-3) \\ -9 - (-7) \end{pmatrix} = \begin{pmatrix} 5 \\ -2 \end{pmatrix}$. Therefore, $m = 5, n = -2$ and $639 + n = 639 - 2 = 637$
3. $\mathbf{d} = \mathbf{a} + 2\mathbf{b}$. Therefore, $k = 1, n = 2$ and $16 - n = 16 - 2 = 14$
4. $\overrightarrow{AB} = \overrightarrow{AO} + \overrightarrow{OB} = -6\mathbf{a} + 4\mathbf{b}$ and $\overrightarrow{OC} = \overrightarrow{OA} + \overrightarrow{AC} = \overrightarrow{OA} + \frac{1}{2}\overrightarrow{AB} = 6\mathbf{a} + \frac{1}{2}(-6\mathbf{a} + 4\mathbf{b}) = 3\mathbf{a} + 2\mathbf{b}$.
   Therefore, $k = 3, n = 2$ and $k \times 7 = 3 \times 7 = 21$
5. $\overrightarrow{CA} = \overrightarrow{CO} + \overrightarrow{OA} = -25\mathbf{b} - 10\mathbf{a} = -10\mathbf{a} - 25\mathbf{b}$. Therefore, $k = -10, n = -25$ and
   $3(k - n) = 3(-10 - (-25)) = 3(15) = 45$
7. $\overrightarrow{BC} = \overrightarrow{BA} + \overrightarrow{AO} + \overrightarrow{OC} = -8\mathbf{a} + 5\mathbf{b} + 11\mathbf{a} = 3\mathbf{a} + 5\mathbf{b}$. Therefore, $k = 3, n = 5$ and
   $n \times 20 = 5 \times 20 = 100$
8. $\overrightarrow{YZ} = 756\mathbf{a} = 252(3\mathbf{a}) = 252\overrightarrow{WX}$. Therefore, $\overrightarrow{YZ}$ is 252 times longer than $\overrightarrow{WX}$
9. After the translation, shape W has corners at coordinates $(4, 0), (4, 1)$ and $(6, 0)$. The bottom left corner of shape W is at coordinates $(4, 0)$. Therefore, $4 \times 724 = 2896$
11. After the reflection, shape X has corners at coordinates $(1, 1), (1, 2)$ and $(-1, 1)$. The top right corner of shape X is at coordinates $(1, 2)$. Therefore, $2 + 479 = 481$
13. The two corner points on shape X that remain in the same position are $(1, 1)$ and $(1, 2)$. Hence, the number of invariant points is 2. Therefore, $88 - 2 = 86$
14. After the rotation, shape Y has corners at coordinates $(-2, 1), (-1, 1)$ and $(-1, 3)$. The largest y-coordinate on the perimeter of Y occurs at coordinates $(-1, 3)$. Therefore, $3 \times 30 = 90$
16. After the enlargement, shape Z has corners at coordinates $(2, 2), (6, 2)$ and $(2, 4)$. The bottom right corner of shape Z is at coordinates $(6, 2)$. Therefore, $6 \times 7 = 42$

Crossword 19

	1			2		3	
	3	■	■	1	9	4	2
	4		5		■		■
	1	6	5	2	■	4	■
		■		■	6		7
	4	■	3	■	2	7	2
	■	8		9		■	
	■	9	8	5	0	■	1
	10		■		■	11	
	9	0	■	6	■	5	■
	■		■	12	13		14
	■	3	■	1	3	7	7
	15			■		■	
	1	1	8	■	3	■	7

Across

2. $A = \pi r^2 \Rightarrow r = \sqrt{\frac{A}{\pi}} = \sqrt{\frac{30}{\pi}} = 3.09..$ m and $C = 2\pi r = 2\pi(3.09..) = 19.416..$ m $= 1942$ cm to the nearest whole number

4. Area of parallelogram $= ah = 28 \times 70 = 1960$ cm².
   Area of semicircle $= \frac{1}{2}\pi r^2 = \frac{1}{2}\pi(14)^2 = 307.87..$ cm².
   Area of shaded region $= 1960 - 307.87.. = 1652$ cm² to the nearest whole number

6. Area of segment $= \frac{71°}{360°} \times \pi(43.05)^2 - \frac{1}{2}(43.05)^2(\sin 71°) = 272$ cm² to the nearest whole number

8. $\frac{85°}{360°} \times \pi(r)^2 - \frac{1}{2}(r)^2(\sin 85°) = 23.64 \Rightarrow 0.74.. r^2 - 0.49.. r^2 = 23.64 \Rightarrow 0.24.. r^2 = 23.64$.
   Therefore, $r^2 = \frac{23.64}{0.24..} \Rightarrow r = \sqrt{\frac{23.64}{0.24..}} = 9.8497..$ m $= 9850$ mm to the nearest whole number

10. The angle in a semicircle (w) is always $90°$

12. Angles in a triangle sum to $180°$. Hence, $x = 180° - (w + 40°) = 180° - (90° + 40°) = 50°$.
    Therefore, $50° \times 27.54 = 1377°$

15. Opposite angles of a cyclic quadrilateral sum to $180°$. Therefore, $z = 180° - 62° = 118°$

Page | 101

Crossword 19 continued

Down

1. $r = \frac{D}{2} = \frac{20}{2} = 10$ cm and $A = \pi r^2 = \pi(10)^2 = 314$ cm² to the nearest whole number
2. Arc length $= \frac{\theta}{360°} \times 2\pi r = \frac{75°}{360°} \times 2\pi(9) = 12$ cm to the nearest whole number
3. Area of sector $= \frac{\theta}{360°} \times \pi r^2 = \frac{75°}{360°} \times \pi(9)^2 = 53.01..$ cm². Therefore, $500 - 53.01.. = 447$ cm² to the nearest whole number
5. Arc length $= \frac{\theta}{360°} \times 2\pi r = \frac{280°}{360°} \times 2\pi(110) = 538$ mm to the nearest whole number
6. Area of sector $= \frac{\theta}{360°} \times \pi r^2 = \frac{280°}{360°} \times \pi(11)^2 = 295.65..$ cm².
Therefore, $316 - 295.65.. = 20$ cm² to the nearest whole number
7. Length of rectangle $= 16$ cm. Diameter of each circle $=$ rectangle length $\div 2 = 16 \div 2 = 8$ cm.
Radius of each circle $= 4$ cm. Width of rectangle $=$ diameter of circle $= 8$ cm.
Area of rectangle $= 16 \times 8 = 128$ cm². Area of each circle $= \pi r^2 = \pi(4)^2 = 50.26..$ cm².
Area of two such circles $= 2 \times 50.26.. = 100.53..$ cm².
Area of shaded region $= 128 - 100.53.. = 27.46..$ cm².
Percentage of rectangle which is shaded $= \frac{27.46..}{128} \times 100 = 21\%$ to the nearest whole number
8. Opposite angles of a cyclic quadrilateral sum to 180°. Hence, $y = 180° - 113° = 67°$.
Therefore, $9098° - 67° = 9031°$
9. As a radius and a tangent always meet at 90°, angle $CTO = ETO = 90°$.
Hence, $a = 90° - 77° = 13°$. Therefore, $548° + 13° = 561°$
11. As $ETO = 90°, b = 90° - 33° = 57°$
13. Due to the alternate segment theorem, angle $c =$ angle ETB. Therefore, $c = 33°$
14. Due to the alternate segment theorem, angle $d =$ angle CTA. Therefore, $d = 77°$

Crossword 20

¹1	3	■	²1	5	³7	■
1	■	⁴2	6	■	⁵2	7
⁶2	⁷1	7	■	⁸5	0	■
■	5	■	⁹4	9	■	¹⁰6
¹¹2	0	¹²2	■	¹³3	4	3
1	■	¹⁴4	9	6	■	1
¹⁵2	5	3	■	6	■	5

Across

1. opp = 9 cm and adj = x. $\tan 35° = \frac{\text{opp}}{\text{adj}} = \frac{9}{x} \Rightarrow x = \frac{9}{\tan 35°} = 13$ cm to the nearest whole number
2. opp = 9 cm and hyp = y. $\sin 35° = \frac{\text{opp}}{\text{hyp}} = \frac{90}{y} \Rightarrow y = \frac{90}{\sin 35°} = 157$ mm to the nearest whole number
4. As angles on a straight line sum to 180°, the smallest angle in the triangle is $\frac{180° - 116°}{2} = 32°$. hyp = 11 cm, adj = x and opp = y. $\cos 32° = \frac{\text{adj}}{\text{hyp}} = \frac{x}{11} \Rightarrow x = 11 \times \cos 32° = 9.32..$ cm. $\sin 32° = \frac{\text{opp}}{\text{hyp}} = \frac{y}{11} \Rightarrow y = 11 \times \sin 32° = 5.82..$ cm. Perimeter = 11 cm + 9.32.. cm + 5.82.. cm = 26 cm to the nearest whole number
5. Area = $\frac{1}{2}xy = \frac{1}{2}(9.32..)(5.82..) = 27$ cm² to the nearest whole number
6. $1 + 72\sqrt{3} \tan 60° = 1 + 72\sqrt{3}(\sqrt{3}) = 1 + 72(3) = 217$
8. $\cos w = \frac{\text{adj}}{\text{hyp}} = \frac{12.8}{20} = 0.64 \Rightarrow w = \cos^{-1}(0.64) = 50°$ to the nearest whole number
9. $a = 32, A = 40°, b = x, B = 79°$. Hence, $\frac{a}{\sin A} = \frac{b}{\sin B} \Rightarrow \frac{32}{\sin 40°} = \frac{x}{\sin 79°} \Rightarrow x = \sin 79° \left(\frac{32}{\sin 40°}\right)$. Therefore, $x = 49$ cm to the nearest whole number
11. $\frac{a}{\sin A} = \frac{b}{\sin B} \Rightarrow \frac{59.36..}{\sin 66°} = \frac{43}{\sin B} \Rightarrow B = \sin^{-1}\left(\frac{43}{59.36..} \times \sin 66°\right) = 41.42..°$. Therefore, $243° - 41.42..° = 202°$ to the nearest whole number
13. Using Pythagoras' theorem $a = \sqrt{(300)^2 + (166)^2} = 343$ mm to the nearest whole number
14. $b = \sqrt{(420)^2 + (264)^2} = 496$ mm to the nearest whole number
15. $c = \sqrt{(570)^2 - (511)^2} = 253$ mm to the nearest whole number

Crossword 20 continued

Down

1. $h = \frac{A}{7} = \frac{84}{7} = 12$ cm. opp $= h = 12$ cm $= 120$ mm and adj $= b$.
   $\tan 47° = \frac{\text{opp}}{\text{adj}} = \frac{120}{b} \Rightarrow b = \frac{120}{\tan 47°} = 112$ mm to the nearest whole number

2. opp $= 12$ cm and hyp $= z$. $\sin 47° = \frac{\text{opp}}{\text{hyp}} = \frac{12}{z} \Rightarrow z = \frac{12}{\sin 47°} = 16$ cm to the nearest whole number

3. $30 \sin 45° + 10 \cos 45° = 30 \left(\frac{\sqrt{2}}{2}\right) + 10 \left(\frac{\sqrt{2}}{2}\right) = 15\sqrt{2} + 5\sqrt{2} = 20\sqrt{2}$. Therefore, $n = 20$ and $n \times 36 = 20 \times 36 = 720$

4. $18 \tan 30° - 6 \sin 60° = 18 \left(\frac{\sqrt{3}}{3}\right) - 6 \left(\frac{\sqrt{3}}{2}\right) = 6\sqrt{3} - 3\sqrt{3} = 3\sqrt{3} = \sqrt{9}\sqrt{3} = \sqrt{9 \times 3} = \sqrt{27}$.
   Therefore, $a = 27$

7. hyp $= 20\sqrt{3}$ cm, adj $= h$ and opp $= b$. $\cos 30° = \frac{\text{adj}}{\text{hyp}} = \frac{h}{20\sqrt{3}} \Rightarrow h = 20\sqrt{3} \times \cos 30° = 20\sqrt{3} \left(\frac{\sqrt{3}}{2}\right)$.
   Therefore, $h = 30$ cm and $\sin 30° = \frac{\text{opp}}{\text{hyp}} = \frac{b}{20\sqrt{3}} \Rightarrow b = 20\sqrt{3} \times \sin 30° = 20\sqrt{3} \left(\frac{1}{2}\right) = 10\sqrt{3}$ cm.
   Area of triangle $= \frac{1}{2}bh = \frac{1}{2}(10\sqrt{3})(30) = 150\sqrt{3}$ cm². Therefore, $m = 150$

8. $a^2 = b^2 + c^2 - (2bc \cos A) = (43)^2 + (62)^2 - 2(43)(62) \cos 66° = 3524.28..$
   $a = \sqrt{3524.28..} = 59.3656..$ m $= 59366$ mm to the nearest whole number

10. Longest side on right-angled triangle (h): $\sin 27° = \frac{\text{opp}}{\text{hyp}} = \frac{41}{h} \Rightarrow h = \frac{41}{\sin 27°} = 90.31..$ m.
    $y^2 = (90)^2 + (90.31..)^2 - 2(90)(90.31..) \cos 41° = 3987.49.. \Rightarrow y = \sqrt{3987.49..} = 63.146..$ m
    $= 6315$ cm to the nearest whole number

11. Horizontal side on T4 found by using Pythagoras' theorem: $\sqrt{(90.31..)^2 - (41)^2} = 80.46..$ m.
    Perimeter $= 90.31.. + 41 + 80.46.. = 212$ m to the nearest whole number

12. Perimeter of T5 $= 90 + 90.31.. + 63.14.. = 243$ m to the nearest whole number

Page | 104

Crossword 21

	1		2	3		4
	1		1	1	2	8
5		6				
7	2	2		0		1
				7	8	
3		2		4	1	3
9	10		11			
5	6	1	3		5	
			12			
	7		7	6	6	
13		14			15	
1		1	5		2	2
16				17		
2	8	0		1	5	

Across

2. Volume = length × breadth × height = $lbh = 18.8 \times 6 \times 10 = 1128$ cm³
5. Surface area = $2(hl + bh + bl) = 2\big((10 \times 18.8) + (6 \times 10) + (6 \times 18.8)\big) = 722$ cm² to the nearest whole number
7. Volume of triangular prism = area of cross-section × length. Area of cross-section = area of triangle. Height of triangle $(h) = \sqrt{6^2 - 3^2} = 5.19..$ cm.
   Area of triangle $= \frac{1}{2}(6)(5.19..) = 15.58..$ cm². Volume = $15.58.. \times 26.5 = 413$ cm³ to the nearest whole number
9. Volume of cone $= \frac{1}{3}\pi r^2 h = \frac{1}{3}\pi(10.3)^2(10) = 1110.97..$ m³.
   Volume of hemisphere $= \frac{1110.97..}{3} = 370.32..$ m³. Volume of hemisphere $= \frac{1}{2}\left(\frac{4}{3}\pi r^3\right) = \frac{2}{3}\pi r^3$.
   Therefore, the radius of the hemisphere, $r = \sqrt[3]{\frac{V}{\frac{2}{3}\pi}} = \sqrt[3]{\frac{370.32..}{\frac{2}{3}\pi}} = 5.6127..$ m = 5613 mm to the nearest whole number
12. Volume of pyramid $= \frac{1}{3} \times$ area of square base × height. Square base area $= \frac{3667}{\frac{1}{3}(30)} = 366.7$ cm².
    Square side length $= \sqrt{366.7} = 19.14..$ cm. Perimeter of square $= 4 \times 19.14.. = 76.59..$ cm.
    Therefore, perimeter = 766 mm to the nearest whole number
14. Surface area of sphere $= 4\pi r^2 = 4\pi(1.1)^2 = 15$ cm² to the nearest whole number
15. Volume of sphere $= \frac{4}{3}\pi r^3 = \frac{4}{3}\pi(1.1)^3 = 5.57..$ cm³. Therefore, $5.57.. \times 4 = 22$ cm³ to the nearest whole number
16. Surface area of sphere $= 4\pi r^2 = 4\pi(4.72)^2 = 280$ cm² to the nearest whole number
17. A pentagonal prism has 15 edges

Crossword 21 continued

Down
1. A cube has 12 edges
3. Volume of cylinder $= \pi r^2 h = \pi(2.5)^2(9) = 176.71..$ cm³.
   Volume of cone = 20% × volume of cylinder $\Rightarrow \frac{1}{3}\pi r^2 h = \frac{1}{3}\pi(1.8)^2 x = \left(\frac{20}{100}\right) \times 176.71..$
   Therefore, $x = \frac{35.34..}{\frac{1}{3}\pi(1.8)^2} = 10.41..$ cm = 104 mm to the nearest whole number
4. Surface area of cylinder $= 2\pi r^2 + 2\pi rh = 2\pi(2.5)^2 + 2\pi(2.5)(9) = 180.64..$ cm².
   Therefore, $180.64.. \times 4.5 = 813$ cm² to the nearest whole number
5. Total surface area of cone $= \pi r^2 + \pi rl$ where l is the slant height on the cone.
   $l = \sqrt{x^2 + (1.8)^2} = \sqrt{(10.41..)^2 + (1.8)^2} = 10.57..$ cm.
   $A = \pi r^2 + \pi rl = \pi(1.8)^2 + \pi(1.8)(10.57..) = 69.95..$ cm².
   Therefore, $69.95.. \times 10.5 = 735$ cm² to the nearest whole number
6. Volume = area of trapezium end face × length $= \frac{1}{2}(2 + 4.6)(2) \times 33.5 = 221$ cm³ to the nearest whole number
8. Side length of square face, $a = \frac{100}{4} = 25$ mm. Volume of cube $= (25)^3 = 15625$ mm³
10. Height of cylinder = total height of solid − radius of hemisphere = 6 − 2 = 4 cm.
    Volume of solid = volume of cylinder + volume of hemisphere $= \pi r^2 h + \frac{2}{3}\pi r^3$.
    Volume of solid $= \pi(2)^2(4) + \frac{2}{3}\pi(2)^3 = 67$ cm³ to the nearest whole number
11. Surface area $= 6a^2 = 6(2.5)^2 = 37.5$ cm². Therefore, $37.5 \times 10 = 375$ cm²
13. A hexagonal prism has 12 vertices
14. An octagonal prism has 10 faces

Crossword 22

	1	2		3		4		5
	1	2	1	5		2	3	3
6								
1		9		6		0		2
7				8				
2	0	0		4	9	3		5
		9				10	11	
6		1	9	0		5	1	
	12				13		14	
	7	0			8		1	9
			15					
	0		1	9	1	3	0	
16		17					18	19
1	8	2	4		4		5	4
				20		21		
7		2		1	6	5		8
7		1		8		6		3

Across

1. x = interior angle size of regular octagon − interior angle size of regular pentagon. Hence, $x = \frac{1080°}{8} - \frac{540°}{5} = 27°$. Therefore, $27° \times 45 = 1215°$

4. $c = 111°$ (as alternate angles are equal) and $e = 180° − 58° = 122°$ (as supplementary angles sum to 180°). Therefore, $c + e = 111° + 122° = 233°$

7. $\vec{AB} = \vec{AO} + \vec{OC} + \vec{CB} = -31\mathbf{a} + 50\mathbf{b} + 35\mathbf{a} = 4\mathbf{a} + 50\mathbf{b}$. Therefore, $k = 4, n = 50$ and $kn = 4 \times 50 = 200$

8. $\vec{DC} = \vec{DB} + \vec{BC} = \frac{1}{2}\vec{AB} + \vec{BC} = \frac{1}{2}(4\mathbf{a} + 50\mathbf{b}) - 35\mathbf{a} = -33\mathbf{a} + 25\mathbf{b}$.
Therefore, $k = -33, n = 25$ and $8.5(n - k) = 8.5(25 - (-33)) = 493$

9. $\vec{ED} = \vec{EB} + \vec{BD} = \frac{3}{5}\vec{CB} + \frac{1}{2}\vec{BA} = \frac{3}{5}(35\mathbf{a}) + \frac{1}{2}(-4\mathbf{a} - 50\mathbf{b}) = 19\mathbf{a} - 25\mathbf{b}$.
Therefore, $k = 19, n = -25$ and $10k = 10(19) = 190$

10. $A = \pi r^2 \Rightarrow r = \sqrt{\frac{A}{\pi}} = \sqrt{\frac{82}{\pi}} = 5.10..$ cm = 51 mm to the nearest whole number

12. Area of sector $= \frac{\theta}{360°} \times \pi r^2 = \frac{150°}{360°} \times \pi(7.3)^2 = 70$ cm² to the nearest whole number

14. Arc length $= \frac{\theta}{360°} \times 2\pi r = \frac{150°}{360°} \times 2\pi(7.3) = 19$ cm to the nearest whole number

15. Arc length $(l) = \frac{\theta}{360°} \times 2\pi r \Rightarrow r = \frac{l}{\frac{\theta}{360°} \times 2\pi} = \frac{450}{\frac{70°}{360°} \times 2\pi} = 368.33..$ cm.
Area of segment $= \frac{\theta}{360°} \times \pi r^2 - \frac{1}{2}r^2 \sin\theta = \frac{70°}{360°} \times \pi(368.33..)^2 - \frac{1}{2}(368.33..)^2 (\sin 70°) =$ 19131.61.. cm² = 19130 cm² to 4 significant figures

16. As the angle at the centre is twice the angle at the circumference, $b = 2(57°) = 114°$.
Therefore, $b \times 16 = 114° \times 16 = 1824°$

18. As a radius and a tangent always meet at 90°, angle $DTO = 90°$.
Hence, angle $OTB = 90° − 69° = 21°$ and reflex angle $AOT = 360° − 114° = 246°$. As angles in a quadrilateral sum to 360°, angle $a = 360° − (57° + 21° + 246°) = 36°$.
Therefore, $36° \times 1.5 = 54°$

20. opp $= y$ and hyp $= 340$ mm. $\sin 29° = \frac{\text{opp}}{\text{hyp}} = \frac{y}{340} \Rightarrow y = \sin 29° \times 340 = 165$ mm to the nearest whole number

Crossword 22 continued

Down

2. Exterior angle of regular hexagon = second largest angle inside right-angled triangle. Hence, exterior angle $= \frac{360°}{n} = \frac{360°}{6} = 60°$ and $a = 180° - (60° + 90°) = 30°$. Therefore, $30° \times 967 = 29010°$

3. Base length of triangle (b) = base length of parallelogram. Therefore, $\frac{1}{2} ab \sin C = \frac{1}{2}(87)(b)(\sin 31°) = 3361$ cm² $\Rightarrow b = \frac{3361}{\frac{1}{2}(87)(\sin 31°)} = 150.01..$ cm.
Area of parallelogram $= bh = (150.01..)(60) = 9001.00..$ cm².
Shaded area $= 9001.00.. - 3361 = 5640$ cm² to the nearest whole number

4. Number of vertices on 210 triangular prisms and 155 square-based pyramids $= (210 \times 6) + (155 \times 5) = 2035$

5. $c^2 = a^2 + b^2 - (2ab \cos C) = (87)^2 + (150.01..)^2 - (2(87)(150.01..) \cos 31°) = 7699.46..$
Hence, $c = \sqrt{7699.46..} = 87.74..$ cm. Therefore, perimeter $= 87 + 150.01.. + 87.74.. = 325$ cm to the nearest whole number

6. After the translation, the largest y-coordinate on the perimeter of shape Q occurs at $y = 2$. Therefore, $2 \times 63 = 126$

11. After the rotation, the largest x-coordinate on the perimeter of shape R occurs at $x = 5$. Therefore, $5 \times 221 = 1105$

12. After the reflection, the largest x-coordinate on the perimeter of shape S occurs at $x = 6$. Therefore, $6 \times 118 = 708$

13. $\frac{a}{\sin A} = \frac{b}{\sin B} \Rightarrow \frac{11360}{\sin 72°} = \frac{x}{\sin 43°} \Rightarrow x = \left(\frac{11360}{\sin 72°}\right) \times \sin 43° = 8146$ mm to the nearest whole number

15. Side length $= \sqrt{9.9} = 3.14..$ cm. Diagonal of square = diameter of circle $= \sqrt{(3.14..)^2 + (3.14..)^2} = 4.44..$ cm. Circumference of circle $= \pi d = \pi(4.44..) = 14$ cm to the nearest whole number

16. Surface area of sphere $= 4\pi r^2 = 4\pi(3.75)^2 = 177$ cm² to the nearest whole number

17. Volume of sphere $= \frac{4}{3}\pi r^3 = \frac{4}{3}\pi(3.75)^3 = 221$ cm³ to the nearest integer

19. Volume of cone $= \frac{1}{3}\pi r^2 h = \frac{1}{3}\pi(6.2)^2(12) = 483$ cm³ to the nearest whole number

20. A hexagonal prism has 18 edges

21. Number of faces on 14 tetrahedrons $= 4 \times 14 = 56$

Crossword 23

1		2		3		4
4	■	8	3	2	■	1
5	6					
2	8	5	■	5	■	2
■		■	7		8	
■	4	■	2	8	8	0
9		10				■
1	■	4	7	■	1	■
11			■	12		
2	5	0	■	2	6	8
	■		■		■	■
7	■	8	■	9	■	■
13		■	14			■
5	6	■	7	5	0	■

Across

2. P(both failing at first attempt) = P(Mike fails first time) × P(Zoya fails first time) = $(1 − 0.74)(1 − 0.68) = 0.0832$. Therefore, $0.0832 \times 10000 = 832$

5. P(Mike passes the test within the first two attempts) = P(pass first time) + P(fail first time but pass second time) = $0.74 + (1 − 0.74)(0.8) = 0.948$. Therefore, $0.948 \times 301 = 285$ to the nearest whole number

7. Expected number of passes = probability of passing × number of people taking the test = $0.72 \times 4000 = 2880$

10. Let x = the number of black pens originally in the box and let y = the number of blue pens originally in the box. Therefore, $\frac{y}{x+y} = \frac{3}{4} \Rightarrow y = 3x$ and $\frac{y-6}{x+y-6} = \frac{5}{7} \Rightarrow 2y = 5x + 12$. Substituting $y = 3x$ into $2y = 5x + 12$ gives $2(3x) = 5x + 12 \Rightarrow x = 12$ and $y = 3(12) = 36$. Total number of pens in the box = $12 + 36 = 48$. As 1 is faulty, 47 are working correctly

11.

		Dice outcome					
		1	2	3	4	5	6
Spinner outcome	1	1	2	3	4	5	6
	2	2	4	6	8	10	12
	3	3	6	9	12	15	18
	4	4	8	12	16	20	24

P(of a product of at least 9. i.e. ≥ 9) = $\frac{10}{24} = \frac{5}{12}$. Therefore, $\frac{5}{12} \times 600 = 250$

12. Numbers 4 and 67 are in set $A \cap B$. Therefore, $4 \times 67 = 268$

13. Numbers 2, 14, 19 and 21 are in set B'. Therefore, $2 + 14 + 19 + 21 = 56$

14. Total numbers = 8. There are 6 numbers in the set $A \cup B$ (3, 4, 14, 19, 67, 123). $P(A \cup B) = \frac{6}{8} = \frac{3}{4} = 0.75$. Therefore, $0.75 \times 1000 = 750$

Crossword 23 continued

Down

1.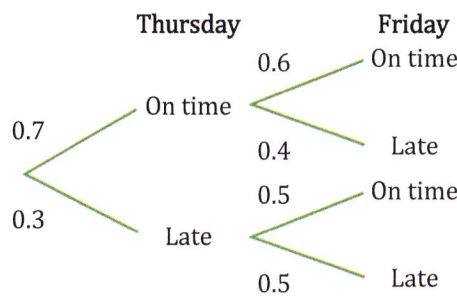

   P(on time on both days) = P(on time on Thursday) × P(on time on Friday) = $0.7 \times 0.6 = 0.42$, which as a percentage is 42%

2. P(on time on at least one day) = 1 − P(late on both days) = $1 - (0.3 \times 0.5) = 0.85$, which as a percentage is 85%

3. P(late on exactly one day) = (P(late on Thursday) × P(on time on Friday)) + (P(on time on Thursday) × P(late on Friday)) = $(0.3 \times 0.5) + (0.7 \times 0.4) = 0.43$, which as a percentage is 43%. Therefore, $43\% \times 6 = 258\%$

4. P(both boxes are green) = $\left(\frac{x}{6+x}\right)\left(\frac{x-1}{6+x-1}\right) = \frac{2}{15} \Rightarrow 15x(x-1) = 2(6+x)(5+x)$.
   After expanding and simplifying: $13x^2 - 37x - 60 = 0 \Rightarrow (13x + 15)(x - 4) = 0$. Therefore, as x is an integer, $x = 4$ and the value of $30x = 30(4) = 120$

6. Probabilities sum to 1. Therefore, $1.25x + 4x + x = 1 \Rightarrow x = 1 \div 6.25 = 0.16$.
   P(not selecting a large paper clip) = 1 − P(selecting a large paper clip) = $1 - x = 1 - 0.16 = 0.84$, which as a percentage is 84%

7. P(first box is red and second is green) = $\frac{6}{10} \times \frac{4}{9} = 27\%$ to the nearest whole number

8. Expected number of medium paper clips = $1275 \times 4x = 1275 \times 4(0.16) = 816$

9. Let A = apples, B = bananas and O = oranges.

   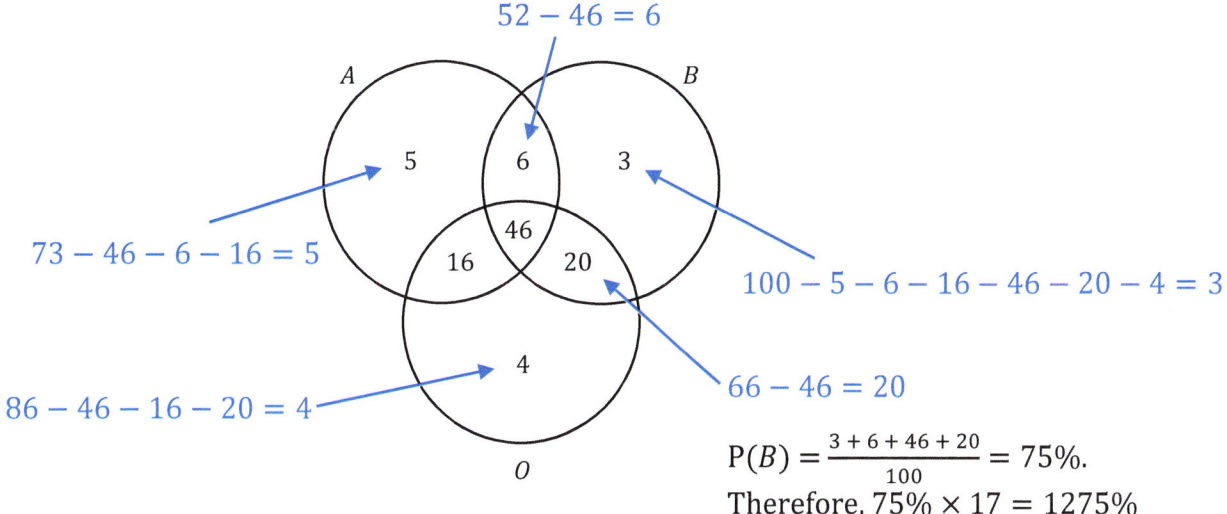

   P(B) = $\frac{3 + 6 + 46 + 20}{100} = 75\%$.
   Therefore, $75\% \times 17 = 1275\%$

10. P(likes only 1 of the 3 fruits) = $\frac{5 + 3 + 4}{100} = 12\%$. Therefore, $12\% \times 34 = 408\%$

12. Number of light bulbs likely to be working correctly = $\frac{5}{6} \times 354 = 295$

Crossword 24

¹2	5	■	²2	2	■	³2
8	■	⁴2	6	■	⁵7	0
⁶5	⁷3	■	⁸9	2	4	■
■	⁹1	9	0	■	¹⁰9	¹¹3
¹²5	8	■	■	¹³3	■	6
8	■	¹⁴1	7	4	0	0
0	■	6	■	5	■	0

Across

1. Mean = sum of values ÷ amount of values.
   Mean = $\frac{(22 + 18 + 40 + 14 + 28 + 23 + 25 + 39 + 22 + 28 + 19 + 22)}{12} = \frac{300}{12} = 25$ minutes
2. Mode = most frequently occurring value = 22 minutes as it occurs 3 times
4. Range = highest value − lowest value = 40 − 14 = 26 minutes
5.

Number of CDs	Number of people (f)	Midpoint (x)	fx
0 to 2	13	1	13
3 to 7	$3c + 1$	5	$15c + 5$
8 to 12	$5c - 4$	10	$50c - 40$
13 to 19	12	16	192
Totals:	$8c + 22$		$65c + 170$

   Mean number of CDs owned = $\frac{\sum fx}{\sum f} = \frac{65c + 170}{8c + 22} = 8$. Hence, $65c + 170 = 8(8c + 22) \Rightarrow c = 6$.
   Therefore, there are $13 + (3(6) + 1) + (5(6) - 4) + 12 = 70$ people in the group
6. Range = highest mark − lowest mark = 59 − 6 = 53
8. Median (Q2) = 28, upper quartile (Q3) = 48, lower quartile (Q1) = 15.
   IQR = Q3 − Q1 = 48 − 15 = 33. Therefore, Q2 × IQR = 28 × 33 = 924
9. 16 members weigh between 50 and 60 kg.
   Frequency = 16, class width = 60 − 50 = 10 and frequency density = $\frac{\text{frequency}}{\text{class width}} = \frac{16}{10} = 1.6$.
   Therefore, each minor interval on the y-axis is worth $\frac{1.6}{8} = 0.2$.

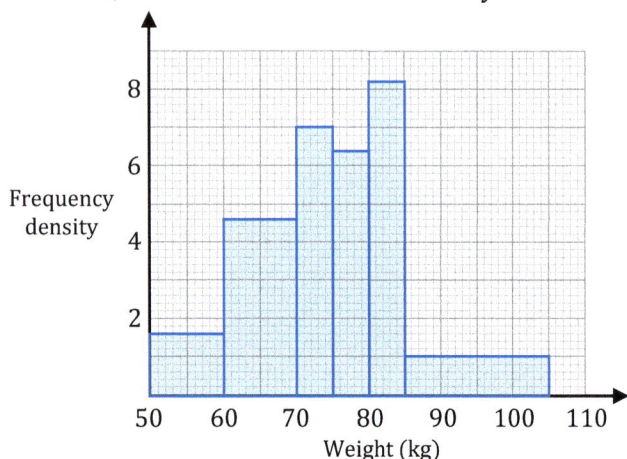

   Frequencies for weight groups calculated using frequency = frequency density × class width:

   50 to 60 kg = 16
   60 to 70 kg = 4.6 × 10 = 46
   70 to 75 kg = 7 × 5 = 35
   75 to 80 kg = 6.4 × 5 = 32
   80 to 85 kg = 8.2 × 5 = 41
   85 to 105 kg = 1 × 20 = 20

   Therefore, the total number of members = 16 + 46 + 35 + 32 + 41 + 20 = 190
10. Number weighing 75 kg or more = 32 + 41 + 20 = 93

Crossword 24 continued

Across continued
12. Number of members weighing between 65 kg and 70 kg = $4.6 \times 5 = 23$. Therefore, an estimate for the number weighing between 65 kg and 75 kg = $23 + 35 = 58$
14. Fraction of sample who said running was their favourite = $\frac{116}{200} = \frac{29}{50}$. Therefore, an estimate for the number at the gym preferring running = $\frac{29}{50} \times 30000 = 17400$

Down
1.

Age group (a) years	Number of people (f)	Midpoint (x)	fx
$10 \leq a < 20$	15	15	225
$20 \leq a < 30$	26	25	650
$30 \leq a < 40$	23	35	805
$40 \leq a < 50$	16	45	720
Totals:	80		2400

Mean age (in years) = $\frac{\sum fx}{\sum f} = \frac{2400}{80} = 30$.
Therefore, $30 \times 9.5 = 285$ years

2. Modal class interval = $20 \leq a < 30$ as it is the single group with the highest number of people within it (26). Hence, $m = 20$ and $n = 30$. Therefore, $20 \times 134.5 = 2690$
3. Times in ascending order: 14, 18, 19, 22, 22, 22, 23, 25, 28, 28, 39, 40. There are an even number of values (12) so the median value will be the $\frac{1}{2}(12 + 1) = 6.5$th value. The 6th value is 22 and the 7th value is 23. Hence, the median (6.5th value) is halfway between the two at 22.5 minutes which is 20 minutes to the nearest 10 minutes
5. Times (hours) in ascending order: 0.3, 0.5, 1.7, 3.2, 4.0, 5.3, 5.7. Lowest value = 0.3, highest value = 5.7, Q1 occurs at the $\frac{1}{4}(n + 1)$ position = $\frac{1}{4}(7 + 1) = 2$nd position = 0.5, Q2 occurs at the $\frac{1}{2}(n + 1)$ position = $\frac{1}{2}(7 + 1) = 4$th position = 3.2 and Q3 occurs at the $\frac{3}{4}(n + 1)$ position = $\frac{3}{4}(7 + 1) = 6$th position = 5.3.

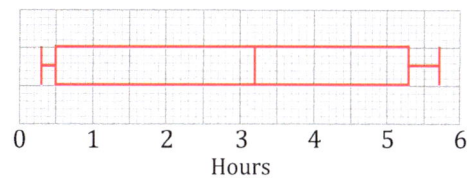

Median (Q2) = 3.2 hours – $3.2 \times 60 - 192$ minutes. Therefore, $941 - 192 = 749$ minutes
7. Q3 = 5.3 hours = $5.3 \times 60 = 318$ minutes
11. Upper quartile value occurs at the $\frac{3}{4} \times 200 = 150$th position. Reading across from 150 on the graph gives a Q3 value of 36 marks. Therefore, $36 \times 100 = 3600$
12. Median value occurs at the $\frac{1}{2} \times 200 = 100$th position. Reading across from 100 on the graph gives a Q2 value of 29 marks. Therefore, $29 \times 20 = 580$
13. The lowest 15% occurs at the $\frac{15}{100} \times 200 = 30$th position. Reading across from 30 on the graph gives a value of 15 marks. Therefore, $15 \times 23 = 345$
14.

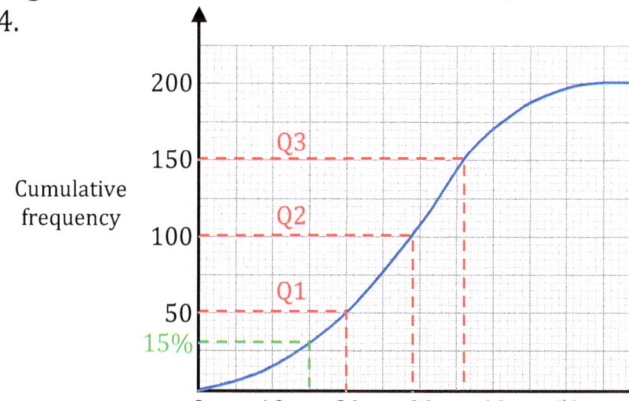

Lower quartile value occurs at the $\frac{1}{4} \times 200 = 50$th position. Reading across from 50 on the graph gives a Q1 value of 20 marks.
Therefore, IQR = Q3 – Q1 = $36 - 20 = 16$

Crossword 25

¹5	²2		³2	⁴1		⁵8	⁷ ⁶6
	⁷9	3		9		1	1
⁸5	0		⁹6	6	7	5	3
	0		7			¹⁰1	8
¹¹5		¹²1	2		¹³1	9	5
		2		¹⁴2	5		4
¹⁵9		¹⁶3	7		0	¹⁷5	¹⁸4
¹⁹6	2	4		²⁰4	5	0	4
0		²¹2	2	8			8

Across

1. P(bus has 2 or more vacant seats on a Monday) = P(2) + P(3) + P(4 or more) = 0.09 + 0.27 + 0.16 = 0.52 = 52%
3. P(sum of vacant seats over 2 days is exactly 3) = P(0 on first day and 3 on second) + P(1 on first day and 2 on second) + P(2 on first day and 1 on second) + P(3 on first day and 0 on second) = (0.35 × 0.27) + (0.13 × 0.09) + (0.09 × 0.13) + (0.27 × 0.35) = 0.2124 = 21% to the nearest whole number
5. On a fair dice P(odd number) = P(even number) = $\frac{3}{6} = \frac{1}{2}$.
   Hence, P(one odd and two even) = P(1st odd, 2nd and 3rd even) + P(1st and 3rd even, 2nd odd) + P(1st and 2nd even, 3rd odd) = $\left(\frac{1}{2} \times \frac{1}{2} \times \frac{1}{2}\right) + \left(\frac{1}{2} \times \frac{1}{2} \times \frac{1}{2}\right) + \left(\frac{1}{2} \times \frac{1}{2} \times \frac{1}{2}\right) = \frac{3}{8}$.
   Therefore, $\frac{3}{8} \times 2336 = 876$
7. P(at least two even numbers) = P(one odd and two even) + P(three even numbers).
   P(one odd and two even) found in clue 5 across as $\frac{3}{8}$. Hence, P(at least two even numbers) = $\frac{3}{8} + \left(\frac{1}{2} \times \frac{1}{2} \times \frac{1}{2}\right) = \frac{4}{8} = \frac{1}{2}$. Therefore, $\frac{1}{2} \times 186 = 93$
8.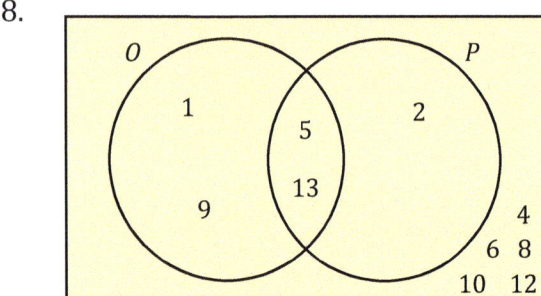
   Numbers 1, 4, 6, 8, 9, 10 and 12 are in set P'.
   Therefore, $1 + 4 + 6 + 8 + 9 + 10 + 12 = 50$
9. Four numbers (1, 5, 9 and 13) are in set O, of which two (5 and 13) are also in the set P.
   Hence, P(member in set P given that member is in set O) = $\frac{2}{4} = \frac{1}{2} = 0.5$.
   Therefore, $0.5 \times 13350 = 6675$
10. Numbers 5 and 13 are in set $O \cap P$. Therefore, $5 + 13 = 18$
11. Median (Q2) age = 28 years. Therefore, $28 \times 179 = 5012$
13. IQR = Q3 − Q1 = 38 − 25 = 13. Therefore, $13 \times 15 = 195$

Crossword 25 continued

Across continued
14. Lower quartile (Q1) = 25 years
16. Range = highest value − lowest value = 47 − 10 = 37 years
17. Frequency = frequency density × class width = 6 × 9 = 54
19. Frequency = frequency density × class width = 24 × 26 = 624
20. Numbers in ascending order: 250, 340, 450, 500, 500. Median is the middle number = 450
21. Mean = $\frac{(240 + 218 + 180 + 167 + 290 + 273)}{6} = \frac{1368}{6} = 228$

Down
2. P(one person has green eyes and the other has brown eyes) =
   P(1st green eyes and 2nd brown eyes) + P(1st brown eyes and 2nd green eyes) =
   $\left(\frac{1}{6} \times \frac{2}{7}\right) + \left(\frac{2}{7} \times \frac{1}{6}\right) = \frac{2}{21}$. Therefore, $\frac{2}{21} \times 304500 = 29000$
4. P(both have brown eyes) = $\frac{2}{7} \times \frac{2}{7} = \frac{4}{49}$. Numerator = 4 and denominator = 49.
   Therefore, $4 \times 49 = 196$
5. P(both cards are the same colour) = P(both orange) + P(both green) + P(both purple) =
   $\left(\frac{16}{30} \times \frac{15}{29}\right) + \left(\frac{6}{30} \times \frac{5}{29}\right) + \left(\frac{8}{30} \times \frac{7}{29}\right) = \frac{163}{435}$. Therefore, $\frac{163}{435} \times 2175 = 815$
6. Number of trains likely to be on time = $\frac{11}{12} \times 6696 = 6138$
9.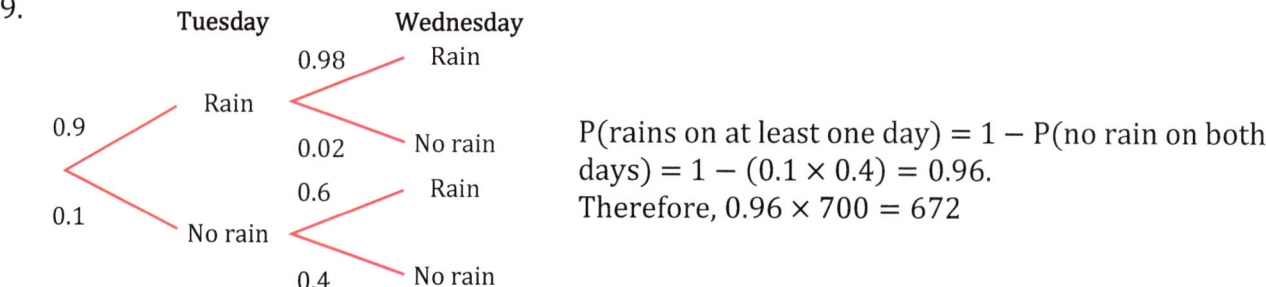

   P(rains on at least one day) = 1 − P(no rain on both days) = 1 − (0.1 × 0.4) = 0.96.
   Therefore, 0.96 × 700 = 672

10. P(both marbles are red) = $\left(\frac{x}{4x}\right)\left(\frac{x-1}{4x-1}\right) = \frac{7}{118} \Rightarrow 118(x-1) = 28(4x-1)$.
    Hence, $6x = 90 \Rightarrow x = 15$. Therefore, $103x = 103(15) = 1545$

12.

Weekly rainfall (r) in mm	Number of weeks (f)	Midpoint (x)	fx
$0 \leq r < 16$	5	8	40
$16 \leq r < 24$	12	20	240
$24 \leq r < 40$	25	32	800
$40 \leq r < 60$	18	50	900
Totals:	60		1980

Mean weekly rainfall (in mm) = $\frac{\Sigma fx}{\Sigma f} = \frac{1980}{60} = 33$.
Therefore, $33 \times 374 = 12342$

13. P(week chosen at random had at least 24 mm of rain) = $\frac{25 + 18}{60} = \frac{43}{60}$.
    Therefore, $\frac{43}{60} \times 2100 = 1505$
15. Modal class interval = $24 \leq r < 40$ as it is the single group with the highest number of weeks within it (25). Hence, $m = 24$ and $n = 40$. Therefore, $mn = 24 \times 40 = 960$
18. The lower quartile is at position $\frac{1}{4} \times 60 = 15$th position in the dataset, which occurs in group $16 \leq r < 24$. Hence, $b = 16$ and $c = 24$. Therefore, $28b = 28 \times 16 = 448$
20. In stratified sampling the proportion of each group within the sample equals the proportion of each group within the population. The proportion of the population which are girls equals $\frac{400}{600 + 400} = \frac{400}{1000} = 0.4$. Therefore, the sample should contain $0.4 \times 120 = 48$ girls